by PARENTS' NURSERY SCHOOL

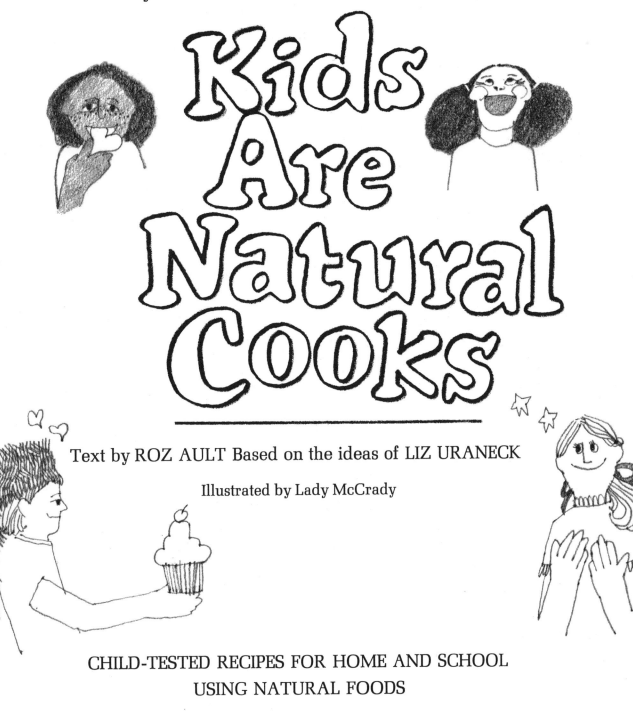

Kids Are Natural Cooks

Text by ROZ AULT Based on the ideas of LIZ URANECK

Illustrated by Lady McCrady

CHILD-TESTED RECIPES FOR HOME AND SCHOOL
USING NATURAL FOODS

HOUGHTON MIFFLIN COMPANY   BOSTON/1974

Library of Congress Cataloging in Publication Data

Parents' Nursery School.
   Kids are natural cooks.

   SUMMARY: Presents a variety of simple recipes
based on natural foods with information on nutrition
and basic cooking techniques.
   1. Cookery--Juvenile literature. (1. Cookery)
I. Ault, Roz. II. McCrady, Lady, illus. III. Title.
TX652.5.P37 1974   641.5   73-22054
ISBN 0-395-18508-4
ISBN 0-395-18521-1 (pbk.)

ACKNOWLEDGMENTS

Cooking, it's been said, is a labor of love; and this book represents the labor and the love of many people — parents, teachers, and children — involved in its creation. Special credit should go to Hap Tierney and Susy Curtis, teachers at the Parents' Nursery School during the year the cookbook was written. Not only did they contribute many of the ideas, but they helped provide the climate where we could carry them out.

For much inspiration and encouragement we thank Bill Uraneck (author and publisher of *The Young Thinker, A Creative Workbook for Children from Five to Ten*).

Among parents who shared recipes and ideas are Barbara Plakans, Cathy Tennican, Miep Kaempfer, Nancy McBride, and Jean Lokensgard. For special contributions of expertise and advice we thank Bob Filene, Chuck and Ruth Smiler, and George Cushing. Others who helped with the project were Diane Mercer and Lucy Baer.

Most important, we thank all the children and all the parents who helped to make Parents' Nursery School a place where kids really can be natural cooks — and create this tangible expression of the cooperative school experience.

CONTENTS

FOR YOU

COOKING WITH CHILDREN THE NATURAL WAY

Based on several years of experiences at Parents' Nursery School, this cookbook takes the simple and familiar and expands it in many directions. Going beyond the readymade product, children learn that not all soup comes from cans, nor bread from packages, nor peanut butter from jars. Cooking does not always start in the kitchen; ingredients are traced right back to the earth where possible, then seeds saved and planted to start the whole cycle over again. Organized around a natural calendar, recipes are tied in with seasonal foods or suggest dishes especially appropriate for each time of the year.

There is a tremendous amount of learning involved in cooking — motor, sensory, conceptual, and social skills all have a part to play. And of special interest to parents are the nutritional benefits in an approach to cooking which stresses natural processes and wholesome ingredients. These recipes are fun to make and good for you — and generally, when children make them they eat them!

All the recipes are clearly arranged and illustrated, and all have been tested with children as cooks. In addition, there is an appendix for teachers and parents explaining the how and why of this kind of cooking, with special attention given to safety tips and pointers for classroom use. Suitable for preschool through elementary-grade children, KIDS ARE NATURAL COOKS is full of ideas for happy learning and good eating.

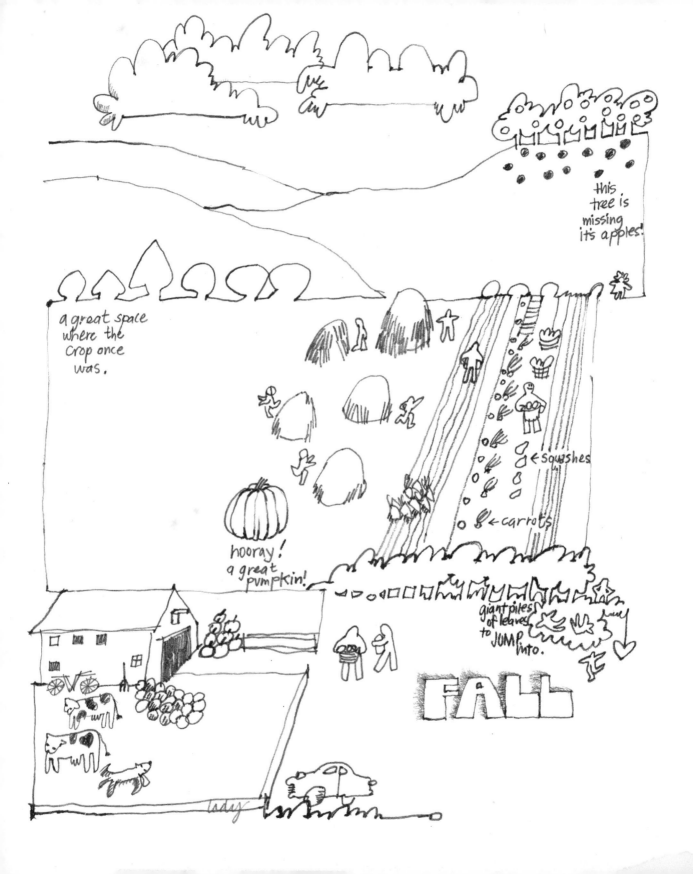

this tree is missing it's apples!

a great space where the crop once was.

hooray! a great pumpkin!

←squashes

←carrots

giant piles of leaves to JUMP into.

FALL

lady

FALL

Fall is a time for visits to farms and gardens, to gather and prepare the harvest.

Fall is a time for apples, for making applesauce and cider.

Fall is a time for picking corn, including popcorn to dry before popping.

Fall is a time for picking carrots, for carrot salad, and squashes, like pumpkins, for pie.

Fall is a time for grains, for grinding into flours and baking into cakes and breads.

Fall is a time for nuts, for grinding into spreads.

Fall is a time for seeds — we cook them, make seed pictures, plant them, and sprout them.

Fall is a time for gathering leaves, such as mint and herbs, and drying them for making tea.

disguised
giant
worm
became great
when he ate
3 apples
in a row.

APPLESAUCE

The best time to make applesauce is in the fall, when the apples have just ripened on the trees. If you live near an apple orchard, sometimes you can even go and pick your own.

There are many different kinds of apples, each with its own fancy name, such as Delicious, Baldwin, Jonathan, Northern Spy, Rome Beauty, and lots of others. You can use just about any kind to make applesauce. McIntosh apples are very good, and usually easy to find.

You will need about one pound of **APPLES** for every cup of applesauce you want to make.

Cut each apple into four pieces. Put the pieces (peels, seeds, and all) into a big pan or an electric skillet.

Cook the apples over medium heat, stirring from time to time, until they are squishy. If the mixture seems too dry or the apples start to stick, you can add a little **WATER,** but fresh apples will usually have enough juice of their own.

Put the apples through a food mill to get rid of all the lumpy parts.

Taste the applesauce and add a little **HONEY** if you like it sweeter.

You can also add a little **LEMON JUICE** to bring out the flavor.

Then sprinkle on a bit of **CINNAMON and NUTMEG.** Stir it all up and eat it, either warm or cooled.

COOKING A PUMPKIN

When Hallowe'en time comes around, buy two pumpkins (if you don't have any in your garden). Make a jack-o'-lantern out of one. The other one you can eat. From one fairly small pumpkin you'll get enough for a pie and some pumpkin bread.

Also, don't forget the seeds. Salt them and roast them, and they make a delicious crunchy snack.

First, here's how you cook the pumpkin:

Cut it in half with a big knife. Inside, you'll see lots of stringy stuff, mixed in with the seeds. Reach in with your fingers and start pulling out the seeds, to separate them from the strings. Put the seeds in a bowl.

When you have most of the seeds out, start scraping out the strings, where they are attached to the pumpkin. You can use a blunt knife and a big spoon to do this. Get all the strings out, and pick out any more seeds you can find.

The part of the pumpkin you want to cook is what is left after all the strings and seeds are taken out. Cut this up into several pieces.

Put the pieces of pumpkin in a steamer (this can be a colander or big strainer set inside a pot). Put water in the pot just up to the bottom of the strainer. Cover the pot, heat it until the water boils, and cook over fairly high heat for about 30 to 45 minutes.

Check every 10 minutes or so, to be sure the water isn't about to boil away. (If it does, you'll have a scorched pot.) Add a little more water if you need it.

When the pumpkin is cooked enough, it should be nice and soft, and the orange skin on the outside should be turning brownish and starting to peel off. Take the pot off the stove.

Then put the cooked pumpkin through a food mill to get out all the lumpy parts. Now it's ready to use in your pie or bread.

NOTE: When you buy a pumpkin for cooking, make sure it is a "sugar pumpkin," grown specifically for eating. Many varieties of pumpkins are only for decoration and won't cook properly. You can't always tell the difference from the outside, so ask the person selling them.

1. cut it open.

oh goodie neat stuff inside.

2. take out the seeds and the strings.

You can't cook JACK O LANTERN

pumpkin's cookin' in the pumpkin pot.

3 cut it up and 4 cook it till it's soft.

5 put it through the mill.

but what can ya do with it?

PUMPKIN PIE CRUST

Here's an easy recipe for a crust that doesn't have to be rolled out with a rolling pin. You mix it right in the pie pan.

Preheat the oven to 400°.

Put a flour sifter in the middle of a 9-inch pie pan. Measure into the sifter:

> 1½ **cups FLOUR (whole-wheat or unbleached)**
> ½ **teaspoon SALT**
> **1 tablespoon BROWN SUGAR**

Sift these things into the pie pan.

Pour into a measuring cup:

> ½ **cup VEGETABLE OIL**
> **2 tablespoons MILK**

Pour the oil and milk into the flour and mix it up with a fork or your fingers, until the flour is all mixed in. Pat the dough out to cover the bottom and sides of the pie pan.

Put the pastry in the refrigerator while you make the filling.

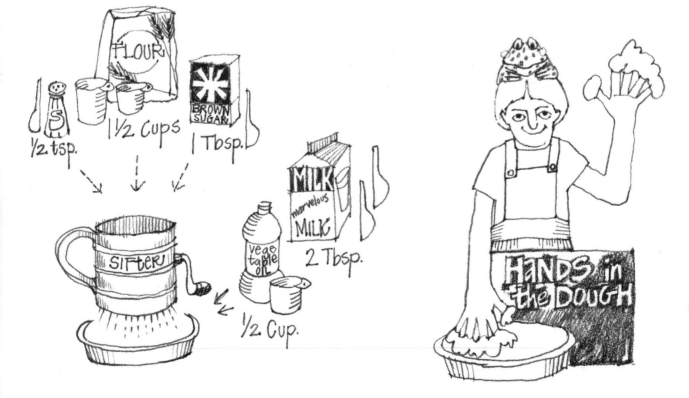

PUMPKIN PIE FILLING

First you need **3 EGGS.**

Crack two eggs and put them in a big bowl. The third one, you want to separate — that means to take the yolk away from the white. An easy way to do this is to first break the egg into a little cup. (Be careful not to break the yolk.) Cup one hand and hold it over a small bowl. Pour the egg through your fingers. The white will slide down into the bowl, and the yolk will stay in your fingers.

Put the yolk in the big bowl with the other two eggs. Save the white for later.

Mix in with the eggs:

> 1½ **cups COOKED PUMPKIN**
> ½ **cup MOLASSES**
> ½ **cup BROWN SUGAR**
> 1½ **teaspoons CINNAMON**
> 1 **teaspoon other SPICES (any mixture of NUTMEG, CLOVES, GINGER, ALLSPICE)**
> ½ **teaspoon SALT**
> 1 **large can (13 ounces) EVAPORATED MILK**
> 1 **teaspoon VANILLA**

Stir this up well with a spoon or egg beater.

Take the pie crust out of the refrigerator. Use a little brush to paint it all over with the egg white you saved. (This helps keep the crust from getting soggy.)

Pour the pumpkin filling into the crust. Bake the pie at 400° for about 50 or 60 minutes. When it is done, you should be able to stick a knife into the filling and have it come out clean, with no pumpkin sticking to it. Let the pie cool before you cut it.

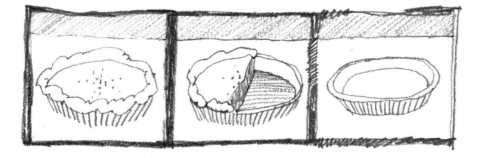

PUMPKIN SEEDS

Before roasting pumpkin seeds, it's a good idea to steam them. That softens the outside part of the seed, so it isn't tough.

First, wash the seeds to get rid of any pumpkin strings that might be stuck to them.

Then put them in a steamer (a pan with holes, inside another pan). Cook them the same way you do the pumpkin meat. The idea is that you want the steam to cook the seeds, but you don't want the seeds to be *in* the water because that washes some of the vitamins out.

Keep the pot covered and cook for about 30 minutes. Add more water when you need it.

Then dump the seeds on a paper towel and pat them dry. Spread them out on a cookie sheet.

Pour on a little **VEGETABLE OIL** — just enough to make the seeds shiny when you stir them around.

Sprinkle on some **SALT.**

Put the seeds in an oven set at 300° for about half an hour till they are golden brown and crispy.

Steam them. Then toast them.

If you can guess how many seeds are in the GREAT PUMPKIN you will WIN them all.

entries here

PUMPKIN BREAD

This is a sweet bread — actually almost a cake. This recipe makes two loaves. If you don't want to eat both of them right away, put one in the freezer.

Preheat the oven to 350°.

Break into a large mixing bowl **4 EGGS.**

Beat them with an egg beater till they look fluffy. Then beat in:

> **½ cup WATER**
> **1 cup VEGETABLE OIL**
> **1 cup COOKED PUMPKIN**
> **1¼ cups MOLASSES**
> **1 cup BROWN SUGAR**

Sift in:

> **3 cups WHOLE-WHEAT FLOUR**
> **1½ teaspoons SALT**
> **2 teaspoons BAKING SODA**
> **2 teaspoons CINNAMON**
> **1 teaspoon NUTMEG**
> **½ teaspoon CLOVES**

Stir everything together till the batter is smooth.

Butter two loaf pans, and pour the batter into them. (They should be about two-thirds full.)

Bake the bread for 45 minutes to an hour. Let it cool in the pans for at least 15 minutes before you take it out.

a beautiful bread.

shout hooray rebeka.

hooray

MY TEACHER'S WEDDING CAKE

Susy, one of our teachers at Parents' Nursery School, got married during the summer. When she came back in the fall, she showed us how she had made her wedding cake, and we all made one together.

Preheat the oven to 350°.

First, you need **2 cups WHOLE-WHEAT FLOUR.**

(We ground our own whole-wheat flour from whole-wheat berries, but you can use pre-ground flour.)

Mix with the flour:

> **1 cup BROWN SUGAR**
> **1 cup YOGURT**
> **1 teaspoon CINNAMON**
> **1 teaspoon NUTMEG**
> **1 teaspoon CLOVES**

Measure **1 cup HOT WATER.**

Stir into the water **1 teaspoon BAKING SODA.**

When the soda is dissolved, pour the water into the flour mixture and stir it up.

Butter a 9-inch pan, and pour the batter into it.

Bake it for about 45 minutes.

When the cake is cooled, you can frost it any way you like. We decided to use lemon frosting. For this, we mixed together:

> **½ stick SOFT BUTTER**
> **POWDERED SUGAR — till it tasted sweet enough (about 1 cup)**
> **LEMON JUICE — squeezed out of one lemon**

CARROT SALAD

We made this salad at school after a trip to a farm, where we picked the carrots.

First, scrub the **CARROTS** well, but leave the skins on.

Grate them into a big bowl.

Mix in a couple of handfuls of **RAISINS.**

Squeeze the **juice from a LEMON** over the mixture. (Use only half a lemon if you don't have many carrots.)

Pour some **HONEY or CORN SYRUP** over the salad until it tastes just right.

GRANOLA

This recipe makes a lot — about 4 quarts. But this crunchy cereal is so good that it probably won't last very long.

Preheat the oven to 275°.

Pour into a very big bowl all the **dry** things and mix them up well:

> **1 box OATMEAL (about 1 pound)**
> **1 jar WHEAT GERM (about 12 ounces)**
> **1 small package COCONUT (about 3 ounces)**
> **2 handfuls SESAME SEEDS (about ¼ cup)**
> **1 teaspoon SALT**
> **1 tablespoon CINNAMON**

You can add other crunchy things you might like, such as:

> **CHOPPED NUTS (about ½ cup — almonds are especially good)**
> **SUNFLOWER SEEDS (about ¼ cup)**

Next add the **wet** things:

> **1 jar HONEY (12 ounces)**
> **⅓ cup SALAD OIL**
> **1 tablespoon VANILLA**

Mix everything well into a big sticky mess.

Put half the mixture into one cookie pan and half in another cookie pan. Pat it out into the corners of each one so it fills the whole pan.

Put the cookie sheets in the oven and bake for about 45 minutes, until the granola is golden brown. (While it's baking, you can wash the bowl and put things away.)

Let the granola cool on the cookie sheets for 5 or 10 minutes, until it is still warm but not too hot to touch. Then stir it up. (If you let it cool too long without stirring, it will get hard and solid — sort of like a giant cookie. That won't hurt anything, but it will be harder to crumble it up.) After it is all cooled, store the granola in a container with a tight cover, so that it stays crisp. Empty coffee cans are good. Or you can put it in a plastic bag.

You can eat granola for breakfast or a snack, with milk and fruit. You can also use it to make other good things. Some recipes in this book which use granola are Crunchy Cookies and Yogurt Sundaes.

14

Grains:
OAT MEAL
Wheat Germ

Nuts and Seeds:
CocoNut

Seasonings:
CINNAMON

Add wet things:
Honey
OIL
VAN ILLA

Bake on Cookie Sheets

Keep it Covered.
Granola
Granola
CANDY

rather, UNDER COVER!

CRUNCHY COOKIES

You can make these with raisins or with chocolate chips. Either way they're delicious.

First, preheat the oven to 350°.

Put in a large bowl:

> **⅓ cup soft BUTTER**
> **½ cup HONEY**

Mix them up well with a wooden spoon or an egg beater until there are no lumps. Then stir in:

> **1 EGG**
> **1 teaspoon VANILLA**

Sift together:

> **1¼ cups WHOLE-WHEAT FLOUR**
> **½ teaspoon BAKING SODA**
> **¾ teaspoon SALT**
> **1 teaspoon CINNAMON**

Pour the flour mixture into the butter mixture and stir it all up well, until you can't see any more flour. Then add:

> **1 cup CHOCOLATE CHIPS or RAISINS**
> **1 cup GRANOLA or CHOPPED NUTS**

Mix everything together and drop teaspoonfuls of dough on cookie sheets (ungreased).

Bake about 10 or 12 minutes, until the cookies are golden brown.

Take the cookies off the baking sheets with a spatula, and let them cool. Makes about 48 cookies.

SPROUTS

You can grow sprouts from almost any kind of grain or dried bean. It takes only a few days and is the easiest possible way to raise your own fresh vegetables.

One of the best kinds to start with is mung beans. These grow into the bean sprouts used in Chinese cooking. You can buy the little green dried mung beans in a health-food store.

Rinse out a one-quart jar and put in it about

3 or 4 tablespoons MUNG BEANS

Fill the jar about half full of water and let it sit in a dark, fairly warm place overnight.

The next morning put a piece of cheesecloth over the top of the jar and hold it in place with a rubber band. Pour off the water and rinse the beans well with fresh water.

You will notice that the beans have grown bigger overnight and their skins may be splitting.

Now all you have to do is keep the beans in the jar in a dark place and rinse them off in the morning and at night. You should drain off the water well each time you rinse them, so that they stay just a little moist but not soaking wet. If you store the jar on its side, the sprouts will have a little more room to grow.

Three or four days after you started them the sprouts will have grown to about one inch or one and a half inches long, and they are ready to eat.

You can try sprouting many other kinds of seeds, such as whole-wheat, soybeans, alfalfa, barley, sunflower seeds, etc. Just make sure you buy seeds that are meant for eating, not planting, so they haven't been treated with harmful chemicals.

You can eat sprouts plain or try some of the recipes in this book that use them. Or you can think up your own ways of fixing them.

Sprouts, by the way, are one of the most nutritious foods in the world, and one of the cheapest, since one pound of seeds will give you six to eight pounds of sprouts. They are loaded with proteins and just about every kind of vitamin and mineral.

WHAT CAN YOU DO WITH SPROUTS?

wee sprout salads

Cook them in a little oil or butter for a few minutes, with some onion and peppers.

Put them in salads.

Grind them up and add to batter for bread, muffins, pancakes, etc.

Make candy — grind them with dried fruit and nuts, mix with honey and spices, roll in grated coconut.

Put them in sandwich spreads. Or make a "Cheese Dream" sandwich: Cover a piece of bread with sprouts, top with sliced or grated cheese, broil till cheese melts. Delicious!

Add your own ideas here:

CORN PONES

Corn cakes like this are most often made in the South, but the recipe goes back to the Indians. "Pone" comes from an Indian word meaning "bake."

You must be sure to use stone ground or water ground whole grain cornmeal (available in health-food stores if your market doesn't carry it). Either white or yellow cornmeal is okay, but DON'T use anything that says "degerminated" on the package. That doesn't mean they've taken out germs; it means part of the grain has been removed, and the cornmeal is pretty tasteless, as well as less nutritious.

Preheat the oven to 400°.

Put in a pan and heat until it boils: **1¼ cups WATER.**

Meanwhile, measure out the dry ingredients:

> **2½ cups STONE GROUND CORNMEAL**
> **1 teaspoon SALT**

When the water is boiling, pour it into the cornmeal and stir it around till it's well mixed in. Then add:

> **¼ cup CORN OIL**
> **¾ cup COLD WATER**

and stir well. The batter should be stiff but not too dry. Add a little more water if needed.

Oil 2 cookie sheets. Then take handfuls of batter and splat them down on the cookie sheets to make little flat cakes. You should have a dozen cakes three inches around or so; more if you make them smaller.

You can, if you like, sprinkle the tops with **SESAME SEEDS.** (The Indians didn't use them, but they do add an extra-delicious crunch.)

Bake the pones 45 minutes, till they're brown around the edges. Serve them hot with butter and jelly.

GRAPE JELLY

Here's how we made grape jelly at school one fall.

First day: We went on a field trip where we picked grapes from a parent's grapevines. We brought back about **2 pounds CONCORD GRAPES.**

Second day: Take the stems off the grapes and wash them. Put them in a pan, crush them, and boil for about 3 minutes. Pour the juice through a jelly bag made of about four layers of cheesecloth into a large container. (This is a job for two adults — one to pour and one to hold the bag.) A good container is a widemouthed gallon glass jar, so you can see the juice. Let the jar sit in a cool place overnight.

Third day: Cut up **5 or 6 APPLES.** Cook the apples over medium low heat till they are soft. Then put them through a food mill. Take the skins out of the food mill and put them back in the cooking pan with **1 cup WATER.** Cook them a second time for about 10 or 15 minutes. Stir in the applesauce (the part that went through the food mill). Then pour the whole apple mixture through the cheesecloth bag into the same jar with the grape juice. Let sit again overnight in a cool place.

Fourth day: Pour the juice out of the jar and measure how much you have. Pour it into a large pan and add ½ **cup SUGAR** for every cup of juice. Heat it, stirring, until it boils; then keep on cooking for about 5 minutes. (It should reach 220° or pass the "jelly test" — fall from the spoon in a sheet rather than in drops.) Then pour it into jelly jars.

If you want to keep the jelly for a long time, you should boil the jars first and cover the tops with wax after putting in the jelly. We didn't bother with that, because we ate ours right away in peanut butter sandwiches.

The amounts we used gave us about 2 pints of jelly. But be sure to allow some extra grapes and apples for eating raw while you cook. You don't need to use any pectin (the stuff you sometimes add to make jelly jell) because there's plenty of natural pectin in the grapes and apple skins.

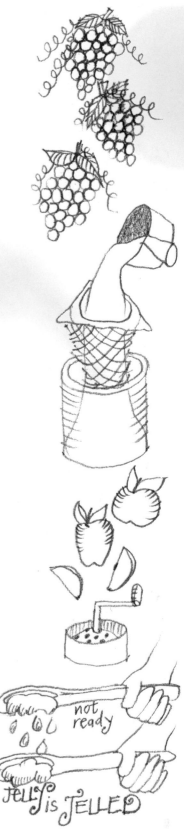

not ready

jelly is JELLED

WHAT can you do with DOUGH?

YOU CAN MAKE SHAPES WITH THE DOUGH AND WHEN IT'S DRIED YOU CAN PAINT IT.

...and put YARN DEEP INTO the DOUGH right before you SHAPE it to make HANGING DECORATIONS.

painted dough doll

PLAY DOUGH

Making play dough can be as much fun as playing with it. Here are two recipes. (You're not supposed to eat these, but there's nothing in them to hurt you.)

Uncooked kind: Put in a big bowl:

> 3 cups FLOUR
> 1 cup SALT
> 2 tablespoons OIL
> 1 cup WATER (add more if you need it)

You can put the bowl on the floor and mix it with your hands till the dough holds together. If it needs more flour, sprinkle some on the table and knead it in.

Now think of all the things you can do with the play dough — pound it, roll it, color it (with food coloring), cut it, stick candles in it. You can add millions of your own ideas.

Cooked kind: Put in a big pan:

> 2 cups COLD WATER
> 1 cup SALT
> 2 cups FLOUR
> 4 teaspoons CREAM OF TARTAR

Cook and stir it over medium low heat for a few minutes until it thickens and looks sort of like mashed potatoes. Dump it out on some waxed paper so it'll cool quickly. (If you want to wait a while before using it, cover it with a damp cloth.) This kind is good for making things you want to keep. You can let it harden overnight and then paint it.

"WOOF WOOF"

BREAD DOUGH

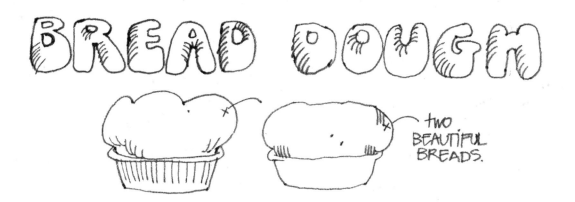

two BEAUTIFUL BREADS.

BREAD DOUGH

Use your favorite recipe. (Double the amount of yeast to shorten the rising time and get finished bread in three hours.)

Here are a few ideas for other things to do with bread dough after the first rising, besides make loaves of bread. You can probably think of some others.

Make **crackers:** Roll dough out thin on floured board. Cut into squares, circles, etc. Bake at 375° on greased cookie sheet 8 or 10 minutes.

Make **fried bread:** Roll dough out (not too thin), cut out shapes. (Or make balls and flatten.) Cook in butter in skillet, turning to brown.

Make **rolls:** Shape balls, let rise and bake in muffin tins. Or make **crescent rolls:** Roll out dough, spread with butter, fold in thirds. Repeat the process; roll out again. Cut out triangles. Roll up toward the point. Let rise and bake on cookie sheets at 325° about 35 minutes.

yum.

Dough Lady

" GRRRR... RUFF "

PEANUT BUTTER

This is a good project for a rainy day, especially if you have plenty of people to help with the shelling.

You will need a bag of roasted **PEANUTS** in their shells.

Crack open the outside shells and take out the peanuts. There will usually be two peanuts in each shell.

Take the thin brown skin off each peanut.

Put the peanuts in a bowl, making sure you don't get any shells in with the peanuts. (Save the shells for mulch or compost.)

When all the peanuts are out of their shells, put them through the finest blade of the food grinder three or more times.

Add just enough **PEANUT OIL** to the ground-up peanuts to make them into a thick paste.

Sprinkle in a little **SALT** until it tastes just right.

Peanut butter made in a grinder will be somewhat chunky — but it still tastes good. If you want it smoother, you'll have to use an electric blender to grind up the nuts. A grain grinder will also give you a smoother spread than a regular food grinder.

Fresh-ground peanut butter is much richer in vitamins than the processed kind you buy in glass jars. However, it also spoils more quickly — so if you plan to keep it more than a day or two, put it in the refrigerator.

You can also experiment with making spreads from other kinds of nuts, such as almonds, cashews, or walnuts, or from sesame seeds.

PEANUT BUTTER PLAY DOUGH

This is even more fun than regular play dough, because you can eat it, and it tastes good.

Take a big jar of **PEANUT BUTTER.**

Spoon out some big globs into a bowl.

Then pour in a few spoonfuls of **HONEY.**

Now add some **POWDERED MILK** (either instant or non-instant type).

Start mixing it all up with your hands. Keep adding the powdered milk until it makes a good dough. For chocolate flavor you can add some **COCOA** or **CAROB POWDER.**

Now you can mold it into any shape you like. Or roll it out and cut out shapes with cookie cutters.

It's also fun to make designs on your shapes with **RAISINS.**

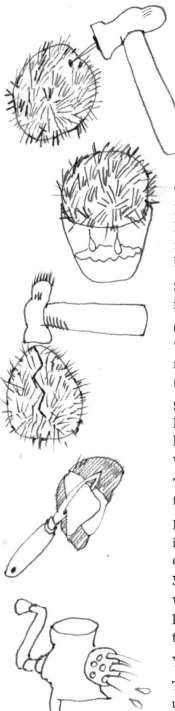

CRACKING A COCONUT

The biggest seed in the world — and one of the tastiest — is a coconut. If you've never seen a coconut growing on a palm tree, you may not know that the coconuts you get in the store have already had one shell removed — an outer greenish husk. But you still have to get through the brown hairy shell to get out the delicious meat. Here's how you do it.

Shake the coconut. You can hear the juice inside sloshing around. The first thing is to get this juice out.

On the bottom of the coconut are three little black spots called the "eyes." (These are where the sprouts and roots come out when the coconut starts growing into a tree.) Hammer a nail into each of these spots (or you can use a pointed screwdriver), and pull it out.

Set the coconut on a small bowl and let the liquid drain out through the holes. Shake it a bit if it's coming slowly. You can drink the juice if you like — it has a mild coconut flavor. (This is NOT coconut milk. That's what you get when you cook grated coconut in water.)

Then put the coconut in a 350° oven for about 30 minutes. This makes the shell easier to crack and separate from the meat.

Let the coconut cool a bit. Then wrap it in a towel on the floor and hit it as hard as you can with a hammer. Keep pounding till the shell cracks. (If you're lucky, you can keep half the shell in one piece, and you'll have a coconut bowl.)

When the shell opens, you can pull it away, or pry it off with a blunt knife. There will be a thin brown skin on the white coconut meat. Peel this off with a vegetable peeler.

You can cut the coconut into little pieces for a chewy snack.

To make grated coconut, put some pieces through a food grinder. (Or use a grater or a blender.) You can sprinkle grated coconut on desserts (toast it in the oven first if you like), or use it in many other recipes.

COCONUT COOKIES

This is a good recipe if you're looking for something to make from a coconut.

Preheat the oven to 350°.

Grind enough fresh coconut to make

2 cups GRATED COCONUT

Set the coconut aside for a few minutes.

Break into a large mixing bowl **2 EGGS.**

Beat the eggs with an eggbeater until they're foamy. Then beat in something to make them sweet. You can use a combination of:

HONEY AND MOLASSES — enough to make 1 cup

OR, you can use **1½ cups BROWN SUGAR.**

Add: **½ teaspoon VANILLA**
¼ teaspoon SALT

Then stir in the grated coconut, along with:

½ cup CHOPPED NUTS or WHEAT GERM

Sift in **6 tablespoons WHOLE-WHEAT FLOUR.**

Stir until all the flour is mixed in.

Butter an 8- or 9-inch square pan. Pour the batter into it. Bake about 30 minutes. Let cool, then cut into squares.

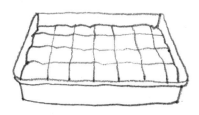

GINGERBREAD

First, preheat the oven to 350°.

Sift together into a bowl:

2 cups WHOLE-WHEAT FLOUR
1½ teaspoons BAKING SODA
½ teaspoon SALT
1 teaspoon GINGER
**1 teaspoon other SPICES (cinnamon, cloves, nutmeg, allspice —
any combination you like)**

Put in a pan and heat on the stove:

1 cup MOLASSES

Take the pan off the stove. Cut into little pieces and stir in

1 stick BUTTER or MARGARINE

Stir it around till the butter melts. If it isn't melting fast enough, put it back on the stove for a minute. Add to the mixture in the pan:

½ cup YOGURT or BUTTERMILK
2 EGGS

You can also add about ½ cup **APPLESAUCE,** if you have any, or some **NUTS** or **RAISINS,** if you want.

Beat the molasses mixture for a minute or so, then pour it into the flour mixture. Stir it just until you can't see any more flour.

Butter an 8- or 9-inch square baking pan. Pour the batter into it and bake about 30 minutes. It's most delicious if you eat it while it's still warm. Good with a little yogurt and honey on top.

SESAME HONEY CANDY

When the ancient Roman soldiers set out for battle, their main food during the long marches was a mixture of sesame seeds and honey. This candy may not make you as strong as a Roman soldier, but it does taste good.

In a big frying pan, over low heat, melt
> **¼ cup BUTTER**

Stir in
> **½ cup SESAME SEEDS**
> **1 cup grated COCONUT**

Stir the mixture around over low heat for about 5 minutes.

Take the pan off the stove. Add:
> **½ teaspoon VANILLA**
> **¼ cup HONEY**

When the honey is all mixed in, put the candy in a cold place till it gets stiff enough to shape into balls. This will take about an hour in the refrigerator or half an hour in the freezer. Or set it in a pan of ice water.

Roll the candy into little balls. You will have about 3 dozen. Keep the ones you don't eat right away in the refrigerator.

BUTTER
½ stick =
¼ cup   +   ½ cup   +   1 cup

½ tsp + ¼ cup

what can you do with POPCORN?

One fall we discovered an organic farm which grew its own popcorn. A group of us went out to pick some ears of popcorn. We brought them back to school and hung them up to dry for several weeks. Finally we scraped the kernels off the ears and popped them.

Even if you don't pick it yourself, popcorn is one of the most fun things you can make and eat. You might also try thinking of some different things to do with it. For example:

1. You can float it in soup.

2. You can shake it in a bag with brown sugar and cinnamon, then mix it in fruit salad.

3. You can grind it in a grinder or blender, then mix it with flour when you bake.

4. You can mix it into some melted chocolate chips, then drop spoonfuls on waxed paper to harden into candy.

5. If you don't feel like eating it, you can use it in collages, or string it with berries to make decorations.

Add your own ideas here:

HALLOWEEN CUTUPS

Everybody makes pumpkin jack-o-lanterns for Halloween. Why not try something different and see how many other kinds of vegetable and fruit cutouts you can make? Six-year-olds and up can do most of this hollowing and cutting by themselves. Here are some of the ones we've used:

  Squash — all kinds, shapes, and colors
  Gourds — ditto
  Apples
  Potatoes
  Onions
  Turnips
  Carrots (fat ones)

At our Halloween party we put all our funny face vegetables in a row and lighted them with tiny blinking Christmas-tree lights.

  We also bobbed for apples in a giant, hollowed-out pumpkin.

  If you have some apples left over, here's a good thing to do with them:

  Take out the cores

  Slice

  String and
  hang to dry

  After a week or so take them down and save them for winter snacks or baking.

ORANGE MINT TEA

On a walk by a pond one fall day, we found mint plants growing wild on the shore. We picked a big grocery sack full and brought them back to school to dry. After a couple of months we made mint tea from the dried leaves and had a tea party.

If you can't find fresh mint, you can buy dried mint leaves at a gourmet or health-food store.

To dry the fresh leaves, put them in a paper bag, fold over the top, and hang the bag in a fairly dry place for several weeks.

This recipe makes enough for a big tea party (about 25 teacups).

First, in a big pan or sink full of water, wash **12 ORANGES** and **2 LEMONS.**

Cut them in half and squeeze out the juice. (The best thing to use is a juicer with a strainer attached to catch the seeds.) Pour the juice into a big pot (at least 4-quart size.)

Rub the peels of the oranges and lemons against a grater until you have shaved off all the rind. (Be sure you get only the thin orange or yellow part on the outside, not the white part underneath, which is bitter.) Add the rind to the juice.

Take the mint leaves off the stems. Crumble the leaves until you have about **1 cup DRIED MINT LEAVES.**

Add the mint to the pot.

Pour in enough **WATER** to make about 3 quarts liquid. Stir.

Heat the tea until it just starts to boil. Then turn the heat to low and simmer it for 15 minutes or so.

Add some **HONEY** — **½ cup or more,** till it tastes sweet enough, and serve.

THANKSGIVING SOUP

Instead of cooking a turkey for Thanksgiving at school, we made a big pot of chicken soup. (This was different from the Vegetable Soup we made later, in the winter, because instead of using a few bones from a big animal, we used a whole chicken.)

After we had looked at the **CHICKEN** and talked about it, we put it in a big pot with enough **WATER** to cover it, and started it boiling.

Meanwhile, we scrubbed and cut up some **VEGETABLES,** peeling the ones that needed it. We put in carrots and celery, and some of the vegetables that people gather in late fall to store for the winter — potatoes, onions, and turnips.

We put in some **HERBS** for extra flavor — bay leaf, parsley, sage, and thyme, plus a pinch or two of **SALT.**

Then we simmered the pot for a couple of hours.

We cooled the steaming hot soup outdoors and served it at the end of the morning to ourselves, our families, and our friends.

WINTER

Winter is a time when we use the freezing outdoor weather for our ice-box, and make gelatins, puddings, and colored fruit ice cubes.

Winter is a time when we make good hot soups, and cool them outdoors before serving.

Winter is a time when we cook with dried fruits, stored to use when fresh ones are not plentiful.

Winter is a time when we make food for the birds.

Winter is a time when we bake cookies and cakes, and frost them for the holidays.

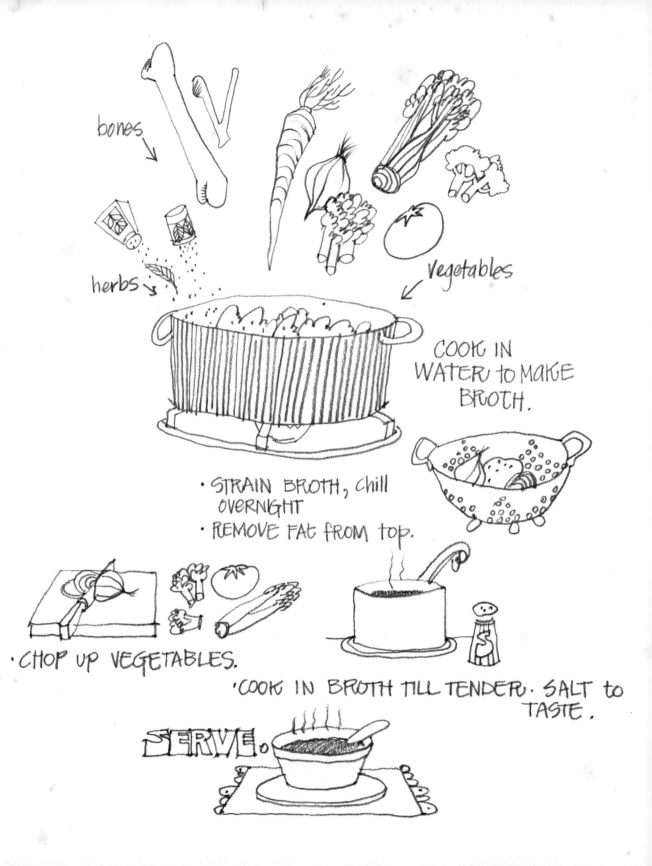

bones

herbs

Vegetables

COOK IN WATER TO MAKE BROTH.

- STRAIN BROTH, chill OVERNIGHT
- REMOVE FAT FROM top.

·CHOP UP VEGETABLES.

·COOK IN BROTH TILL TENDER. SALT to TASTE.

SERVE.

VEGETABLE SOUP

Our school soup-making project evolved from a display of different kinds of bones. After looking at, feeling, and talking about bones, we decided to do some cooking with them.

We started with a walk to a nearby store to buy some soup bones. (Our visit was arranged ahead of time with the butcher.)

On the first day we put the **BEEF BONES** in a big pot.

We added **WATER** to cover the bones.

Then we put in a couple of **VEGETABLES** for flavoring (onion, carrot, celery, etc.), plus some **HERBS** (bay leaf, thyme, parsley, etc.).

A spoonful or two of **VINEGAR** added to the pot helps dissolve the valuable minerals out of the bones and into the soup.

We cooked this mixture slowly for a few hours. Then we put the soup in the refrigerator overnight.

Meanwhile, we talked about what else we could put in the soup. Everyone was encouraged to bring a favorite **VEGETABLE** the next day to add to the pot. Other suggestions were **NOODLES** — especially in interesting shapes, like alphabet noodles.

The second day we looked at the broth that had been chilled overnight. We took off the fat that had collected on the top and talked about why it rose to the top and got hard. Then we heated up the broth again.

We tasted it to see if it needed **SALT.**

We washed and cut up our vegetables. We peeled the ones with tough skins, but left the others unpeeled to save the vitamins.

We put the vegetables and noodles in the boiling soup and cooked it all just until the vegetables were tender.

Before, after, or during soup-making, a good book to read is *Stone Soup,* a very old folk tale about the peasant who made soup from a stone.

DOUBLE DUMPLING SOUP

This soup has little meatballs and little cheese balls floating in it.

The first thing you need is about half a cup of broth for each person you want to serve. For a quick soup, you can use canned broth (a mixture of chicken and beef is especially good). But the best thing is to make your own. To do this, put in a big pot:

Some BONES with MEAT (beef and/or chicken)
Some VEGETABLES: one or two each of a few
different kinds, such as ONIONS, CELERY,
CARROTS, TOMATOES, TURNIPS
Some SEASONINGS: PARSLEY, BAY LEAF,
THYME, MARJORAM, PEPPERCORNS, etc.

Put in enough **WATER** to cover the mixture. Bring it to a boil. Then turn down the heat and cook it over low heat for at least two hours.

Pour the broth through a strainer into another pot. Taste it and add as much **SALT** as you think it needs.

The next thing is to make the dumplings. For the meat dumplings either use raw ground beef, or grind your own cooked leftover meat. If you have made your own broth, you can separate the cooked meat from the bones and grind it in the food grinder. Mix together:

About 1 pound GROUND MEAT
1 EGG
½ teaspoon SALT
BREAD CRUMBS, enough to make a stiff mixture

Shape the meat mixture into little balls (20 or so).

Next, make the cheese dumplings. (These amounts will make about 12 medium-sized dumplings.) Put into a bowl:

2 tablespoons SOFT BUTTER
2 EGGS

Beat this up well, then stir in:

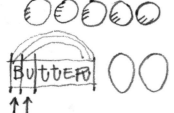

6 tablespoons FLOUR (whole-wheat or unbleached)
½ teaspoon SALT
½ cup GRATED CHEESE

Heat the broth until it is boiling. Then put in the meatballs, and drop in little spoonfuls of the flour batter. Watch the pot, and you will see the dumplings start to float to the top as they finish cooking. They should be ready to eat in about 10 minutes.

TOADS IN HOLES

The "toads" that peek up through the holes in the batter are meatballs. (Sometimes this is made with sausages.)

Preheat the oven to 350°.

Mix together: **1 EGG**
                  1 tablespoon dried ONION FLAKES
                  1 tablespoon SOY SAUCE
                  2 tablespoons KETCHUP
                  1 pound GROUND BEEF

Butter a 9- or 10-inch pie pan. Shape the meat mixture into little balls (about 24) and put them in the pan.

Now make the batter. Beat until foamy:

                3 EGGS

Stir in   **1 cup MILK**
            1 teaspoon SOY SAUCE
            1 tablespoon VEGETABLE OIL

Sift in   **¾ cup UNBLEACHED FLOUR**
            1 teaspoon BAKING POWDER

Stir in   **¼ cup WHEAT GERM**

Pour the batter over the meatballs. Bake about 50 minutes, until the batter is golden and puffy. Serve at once to 4 or 5 hungry people.

FOR the MEATBALLS:

MIX TOGETHER: 1 EGG   ONION FLAKES 1 Tbsp.   SOY SAUCE 1 Tbsp.   KETCHUP 2 Tbsp.   GROUND BEEF 1 POUND

FOR THE BATTER:

3 EGGS • BEAT TILL FOAMY   MILK 1 cup • STIR IN 1 tsp.   SOY SAUCE OIL 1 Tbsp.   FLOUR 3/4 cup • SIFT IN 1 tsp   Wheat Germ 1/4 cup • STIR IN

OATMEAL-RAISIN SOUP

This recipe comes from Norway, where they usually eat the soup with Norwegian Potato Dumplings (see next page).

Start with about **1 quart of WATER.**

Put the water in a big pan and heat it until it boils.
Then stir in:

> **a couple of handfuls of OATMEAL**
> **a couple of handfuls of RAISINS**
> **a pinch or two of SALT**

Then add some **GRAPE JELLY** — enough to make it look purple and taste grape-y.

Keep cooking and stirring until the oatmeal is soft and the raisins are plump.

This makes enough for about 6 or 8 people.

KUMPE

Kumpe is the Norwegian name for Potato Dumplings.

First, boil about 3 medium-sized **POTATOES** in water until they are cooked all the way through. (This will take about 40 minutes for whole potatoes.) Let them cool (you can run cold water over them to speed it up) till they don't burn your fingers. Then peel them.

Meanwhile, peel about **6 RAW POTATOES.**

Put the raw and cooked potatoes through a food grinder together.

Add to the potatoes some **FLOUR (whole-wheat or unbleached)** till it feels right and **SALT** till it tastes right. The dough should be stiff enough to stay together in a ball and should taste pretty salty.

Cut about a pound of **SUET** into little cubes (about ¾-inch).

Shape balls of dough around the pieces of suet.

Heat a big pot of water to boiling. Drop the dumplings into the water and cook them over medium-low heat for about an hour.

Serve them hot with lots of butter. (Don't eat the suet in the middle — save it for the birds.) Makes 8 generous servings.

If there are any dumplings left over, put them in the refrigerator overnight. Then slice them about ½ inch thick and fry them in a little oil or butter. Serve with more butter. Delicious!

peeled potato

• peel and grind cooked and raw potatoes.

FLOUR

• add flour & salt
• make balls around suet pieces.

• BOIL ONE HOUR.

EAT

PIZZA DOUGH

This makes enough for two pizzas. If you don't have pizza pans, you can make one large pizza on a cookie sheet and one small pizza in a pie pan. Or divide the dough into small pieces and let each person make his or her own mini-pizza.

First, make the dough.

Mix together in a large bowl and let stand for five minutes:

1 cup WARM WATER
1 package YEAST
1 tablespoon SALAD OIL
1 teaspoon HONEY
1 teaspoon SALT

Mix and let stand 5 MINUTES:

1 cup WARM WATER   1 pckg YEAST   1 Tbsp.   1 tsp.   1 tsp.

PIZZA DOUGH

catch!

(While you're waiting for the five minutes to pass, you can start cutting up a couple of onions into little pieces, because you'll need them for the sauce.)

After five minutes, stir in **2¼ cups WHOLE-WHEAT FLOUR**

When the flour is well mixed in, shape the dough into a ball. Pour a few drops of **SALAD OIL** into the bowl and turn the ball of dough around in the oil, so that all sides of the dough are coated with the oil. Let the dough sit in a warm place to rise for 45 minutes.

Stir in 2¼ cups Whole Wheat FLOUR

FLAT. after only 15 minutes

A GREAT DOUGH after 45 minutes

Shout HOORAY!

LET it RISE!

PIZZA SAUCE

Meanwhile, make the sauce.

In a large frying pan, crumble up **1½ pounds GROUND BEEF**

Add: **2 chopped ONIONS**
      2 chopped or mashed cloves of GARLIC

Cook this over medium heat, stirring once in a while, until the meat is all browned and no pink is left. Add:

    1 large can TOMATO SAUCE (16 ounces)
    1 large can WHOLE TOMATOES (about 35 ounces) drained
    1 teaspoon SALT
    ½ teaspoon OREGANO
    ½ teaspoon BASIL

Stir the mixture around until the tomatoes are broken up into pieces. Let it cook over medium heat about 15 minutes, stirring it every few minutes.

When the dough has risen, punch it down with your fist. Preheat the oven to 475°.

Sprinkle a little **FLOUR** on a board or clean table. Knead the dough (that means to squeeze it around and mix it with your hands) on the flour until it is nice and smooth. If it seems too sticky, sprinkle on a little more **FLOUR.**

Divide the dough into two parts. Put each one in a pizza pan or other shallow pan and pat it out until it covers the bottom. Cover the dough with the tomato-meat sauce. Cover the sauce with

    ½ pound MOZZARELLA CHEESE, thinly sliced
    ¾ cup PARMESAN CHEESE, grated

Put the pizzas on the bottom rack of the oven and bake them for about 25 minutes, until the crust is browned, the cheese is melted, and the sauce is bubbly.

1½ POUNDS GROUND BEEF

+

2 CHOPPED ONIONS
2 CHOPPED GARLIC CLOVES

ADD: SAUCE 16 OZ. · Red tomatoes 35 OZ.

+ 1 tsp · ½ tsp OREGANO · ½ tsp BASIL

PUNCH the DOUGH DOWN.

OUCH!!

"WE DID IT! RED PIZZAS!!"

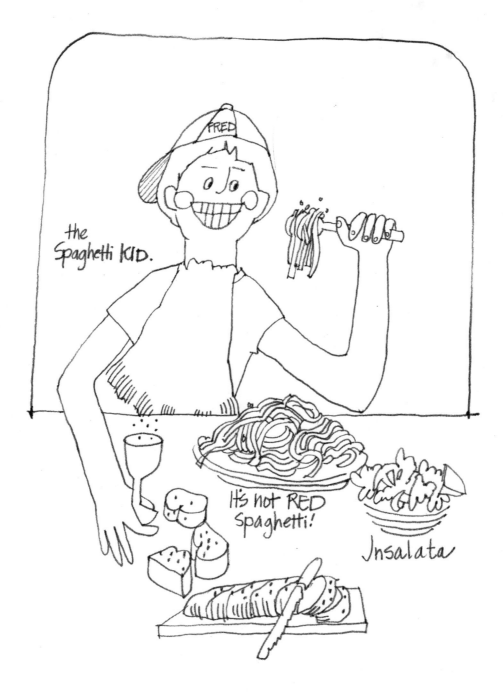

SPAGHETTI
ALLA CARBONARA

This spaghetti is very quick to fix, and a nice change from the usual tomato sauce.

Preheat the oven to 400°.

Cut the slices from **1 pound BACON** into little squares. (You can do this with scissors.)

Then put the squares in some large baking pans, making sure they aren't on top of each other. Bake them in the oven for 15 or 20 minutes, until they are brown and crispy. (Be sure an adult takes the pans out and pours off the hot grease.) Let the bacon pieces drain on paper towels.

Meanwhile, put in a large pan **about 4 quarts WATER.**

Heat the water until it is boiling. Then add **1 pound SPAGHETTI.** (The whole-wheat kind is best.)

Cook the spaghetti for about 10 minutes. While the bacon and spaghetti are cooking, put in a small pan:

> **1 stick (¼ pound) BUTTER**
> **1 peeled clove GARLIC**

Melt the butter over low heat and keep it warm.

Break into a bowl **2 EGGS** and beat them for a minute or so.

Chop enough **PARSLEY to make ⅓ cup.** (You can use scissors here, too.)

When the spaghetti is done, drain it in a colander. Put it in a large bowl.

Take the garlic out of the butter. Pour the butter over the spaghetti and mix it up.

Then pour in the eggs and mix together quickly.

Next, sprinkle on ½ **to ¾ cup grated PARMESAN CHEESE.** Stir again.

Finally, add the bacon pieces and the parsley. Mix everything together, and it's ready to eat. Serves 6.

PORCUPINES

These little meatballs look prickly, but their quills are actually made of rice.

Preheat the oven to 450°.

Put in a big bowl and mix together:

> **1 pound GROUND BEEF**
> **½ cup BROWN RICE (uncooked)**
> **1 EGG**
> **1 tablespoon SALAD OIL**
> **1 small ONION, chopped or grated**
> **1 teaspoon THYME**
> **¾ teaspoon SALT**
> **¼ teaspoon PEPPER**
> **1 tablespoon PARSLEY, chopped**

Shape the meat mixture into little balls. Put them in a pan big enough to hold them all in one layer. Put them in the oven for about 15 minutes, until they are brown.

Then take them out of the oven and pour into the pan **2 cups TOMATO JUICE.**

The balls should be covered by the juice; if they're not, add more juice or a little water.

Cover the pan tightly (use aluminum foil if the pan doesn't have a top). Put it back in the oven, and turn the heat down to 325°. Let them cook for about an hour, until the rice is tender.

• Mix MEAT RICE EGG & SEASONINGS.

• MAKE BALLS

• BROWN THEM 15 MINUTES at 450° ADD LIQUID.

BAKE 325

• BAKE ONE HOUR & SERVE.

PASTA E FAGIOLI

(NOODLES and BEANS)

It's interesting that beans and noodles, which are both pretty good foods by themselves, are better for you if you eat them together. Each of them has part of the proteins you need to build your body, and your body has to get both of them in one meal to put them together in the right way. Cooks from many countries seem to have figured this out by themselves, for there are many old recipes which combine beans with either rice or noodles. This one is from Italy. It's fun to use noodles in fancy shapes, like little bows or shells.

First, cut up: **1 ONION**
2 cloves GARLIC
1 stalk CELERY (with leaves)

Put in a frying pan **4 slices of BACON.** Cook the bacon slowly until it's brown. Then take it out of the frying pan and drain it on paper towels.

Put the cut-up vegetables in the bacon grease and cook them slowly, stirring them around, for 5 minutes. Then put the bacon back in the pan and add **1 large can TOMATOES** (about 35 ounces).

Cook for about 5 minutes. Then stir in:

> **1 can KIDNEY BEANS** (about 1 pound)
> OR
> ½ **pound dried BEANS soaked overnight**

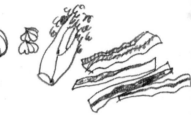

Then add: ⅓ **cup chopped PARSLEY**
½ **teaspoon SALT**
1 teaspoon BASIL

Cook over low heat, covered, for about 1 hour. Then stir in **1 cup un-cooked tiny NOODLES.** Add some **WATER** if the mixture seems too dry.

Cook 10 minutes longer, and serve, with **GRATED CHEESE** if you like. (Makes 4 to 6 servings.)

NOODLES 1 CUP

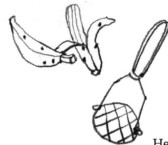

MAKE-YOUR-OWN
INSTANT PUDDING

Here are two quick recipes for pudding that doesn't come out of a box. Either one can be ready to eat in just a few minutes. Each of these makes about 4 servings but can be easily increased. Maybe they'll give you some ideas for, combinations of your own.

FRUIT PUDDING

Peel 2 ripe BANANAS.
(They should have some grown spots on the outside to be ripe enough so they're soft.) Cut them up into little pieces and put the pieces in a pan or bowl with a fairly flat bottom. Mash up the pieces with a potato masher until they're pretty smooth.

Stir in about: **½ cup APPLESAUCE**
2 tablespoons PEANUT BUTTER
2 tablespoons HONEY

The exact amounts aren't too important; you can vary them to suit your tastes. Stir up the pudding till it's smooth enough (a wire whisk is a good thing to use). Serve at once or chill and eat later. You can sprinkle on a little **CINNAMON** if you like.

CHOCOLATE PUDDING

First squeeze the juice out of half a large lemon or a whole small lemon. You should have about
2 or 3 tablespoons LEMON JUICE.

Pour **one small can (5⅓ ounces) EVAPORATED MILK** into a deep bowl or pan. (If you have a chance to chill the milk first, it will whip up thicker, but it will still work if it's not cold.)

Pour the lemon juice into the milk and start beating with an egg beater.

When it's getting thick, start adding **½ cup PRESWEETENED COCOA-MILK POWDER** (the stuff you use to make chocolate milk). Add this a couple of spoonfuls at a time, and keep beating till it's all mixed in and creamy.

Eat the pudding right away or chill it. It's also very good frozen.

WHAT·CAN·YOU·DO·WITH ¿Bananas?

If you make friends with a fruit man, sometime you might have the chance to get, as we did, a huge crate of very ripe bananas for almost nothing. Of course, we had to use them up right away — so we all had to think up suggestions on what to do with bananas. Here are some of our ideas.

BANANA-OATMEAL SOUP

Boil **5 cups WATER** with **1 teaspoon SALT** in it. Pour in **2 cups OAT-MEAL.** Cook 5 minutes. Mash **3 BANANAS** and put them in the oatmeal. Put in some **RAISINS** and serve plain or with milk.

BANANA POPSICLES

Dip **BANANAS** in **CHOCOLATE SYRUP.** Roll them in **GRATED COCONUT, CHOPPED NUTS,** or **GRANOLA.** Freeze several hours.

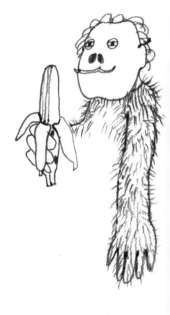

BANANA SANDWICHES

Slice **BANANAS** and make sandwiches with **PEANUT BUTTER** or **CREAM CHEESE.**

BANANA MILKSHAKE

Mash some **BANANAS.** Mix them up with **MILK** and **FRUIT JUICE.**

BANANA PUDDING

See the recipe for fruit pudding on the opposite page.

BRANANA MUFFINS

Preheat oven to 400°.

Mix together   **1 cup ALL-BRAN**
              ¼ cup MILK
              3 mashed BANANAS
              1 EGG
              2 tablespoons VEGETABLE OIL

Sift in   **1 cup FLOUR**
              2½ teaspoons BAKING POWDER
              ½ teaspoon SALT
              ¼ cup SUGAR

Stir quickly (leave some lumps). Fill muffin pans two-thirds full. Bake 30 minutes. Makes 12.

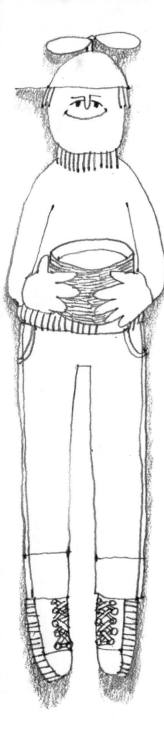

HOME-MADE GELATIN —
THE OLD-FASHIONED WAY

Nowadays, when powdered gelatin arrives at the store in neat little boxes, most people have forgotten where it originally came from. If you look in old cookbooks, you might find recipes for "calves' foot jelly" (supposedly very good for sick people) — and in the days before packaged mixes the only way to get gelatin was to extract it from the bony parts of animals. You might have a little trouble obtaining calves' feet today, but most well-stocked butchers can supply you with pigs' feet, which you can use to make gelatin from the very beginning. When sweetened and flavored with fruit, the end product is delicious, with no "animal" taste.

Plan on three days from start to finish: one day to cook the bones, one day to clarify the gelatin, and a third to chill it before eating.

Pigs' feet are often sold split down the middle lengthwise, which is interesting because you can see the different bones and ligaments inside the foot. Many people have never seen pigs' feet up close, and it's fun to start by asking everyone to guess what they are. Some of the guesses we came up with were "a glove," "a puppet," "a rooster head," and "part of a moose."

Start with **2 or 3 PIGS' FEET.** (You don't need to take off the skin unless it still has hair on it.)

Put the feet in a big pot (at least 4-quart size) and cover with **WATER.** Heat it until it boils. Skim off the foam from the top, then cook slowly for at least 4 hours (until about half the water has boiled away).

Pour the liquid through a strainer to get out the bones and meat. (Save the bones, because if you boil them again, you can get still another batch of gelatin.) You should have about one quart of liquid.

Chill the liquid overnight.

The next day you will see that the liquid has hardened into a solid mass of gelatin. But you still have to get rid of all the parts that aren't supposed to be in the gelatin.

First, scrape off the fat on the top. If there are any little pieces of fat still stuck on, rinse them off quickly with hot water. Then run hot water over the bottom of the pan or bowl until the gelatin is loose enough to dump out onto a plate. Scrape off any bits of meat stuck on the bottom.

Put the gelatin in a pan on the stove over low heat.

Now you have to *clarify* it. This means to get out the stuff that makes it look cloudy. For this you need **5 EGGS.** (You can use fewer eggs if you want, but the gelatin won't be quite as clear.)

Separate the yolks from the whites of the eggs by pouring the egg through your fingers (held just a little bit apart) into a bowl. The white will slide through and the yolk will stay in your fingers. Put the yolks aside and use them in another recipe.

Beat the whites with an egg beater just till they're foamy. Smash up the eggshells (this is one time you want to use the shells) and put the shells and the whites into the warm gelatin as soon as it has melted. (The eggs will soak up the parts you still want to get out of the gelatin.)

Pour in ½ **cup HONEY.** Stir just to mix, and don't stir again. Let the mixture boil for ten minutes. Then add ½ **cup COLD WATER** and boil for 5 minutes more.

Take the pan off the stove, cover it, and let it stand at room temperature for 30 minutes.

Meanwhile, you can be cutting up and squeezing the **FRUITS** you want to add. If you have a quart of gelatin you can add about an equal amount of **FRUIT JUICE** to it. Fresh-squeezed orange juice is best, but you can use frozen or canned. Cut-up apples and bananas are good too — almost any kind of fruit except fresh or frozen pineapple. If you use oranges, add a little **GRATED RIND.**

Line a colander with several layers of cheesecloth and run hot water over it. (This keeps the gelatin from cooling and jelling in the cheesecloth.) Then pour the eggy gelatin through the colander into a bowl. Squeeze the cheesecloth to get all the liquid through. If it still looks pretty cloudy, strain it again.

Now mix the clear liquid with your fruits and fruit juices. Put it in the refrigerator again to chill several hours or overnight.

ORANGE JELL

Making gelatin from bones is fun for a special project, but most of us wouldn't have time to do that very often. When you want a quick gelatin dessert, try this way of doing it. You can make this just as fast as with a presweetened mix, and it will be much more nutritious, as well as fresher tasting.

Put into a pan ½ **cup COLD WATER.**

Sprinkle in **1 package PLAIN GELATIN.**

Cook it over low heat for about three minutes, stirring it all the time, until the gelatin is all dissolved.

Take it off the stove and stir in:

> **1 small can (6 ounces) FROZEN ORANGE JUICE**
> **1 cup COLD WATER**
> **¼ cup HONEY**

Put mixture in the refrigerator until it jells — about two hours.

If you want to, you can add some sliced **FRUIT** — any kind you like.

Stir the fruit in after about half an hour, when the gelatin has just started to get thick.

You can change the flavor by using different kinds of juice. But don't use fresh or frozen pineapple juice unless you cook it first because it will keep the gelatin from getting thick. Canned pineapple juice is okay.

If you want to use fresh or canned juice, instead of frozen, then leave out the water and use a total of two cups of juice.

JAN HAGEL COOKIES

This is a recipe from Holland, given to us by a Dutch mother at Parents' Nursery School. (She changed it a little to use whole-wheat flour.)

Preheat the oven to 350°. Butter a large cookie pan (about 11 x 15 inches).

Put in a big bowl, and mix together with your hands:

> **2 cups WHOLE-WHEAT FLOUR**
> **¾ cup UNBLEACHED WHITE FLOUR**
> **2 sticks (½ pound) soft BUTTER**
> **1 cup DARK BROWN SUGAR**
> **1 tablespoon CINNAMON**
> **½ teaspoon BAKING POWDER**
> **a pinch of SALT**

When it's well mixed, pat the dough on the buttered cookie pan. It should be about ¼ inch thick.

Dip a pastry brush in **WATER** and paint it all over the top of the dough.

Sprinkle the top with **1 cup chopped or ground NUTS.**

Press the nut pieces into the dough.

Bake for about 20 minutes, until the nuts are golden brown.

Cut into squares or diamond shapes while still warm. Let the cookies cool about 10 minutes on the cookie sheet before removing them with a spatula. Then let them cool completely on a plate or rack before putting them into a cookie jar.

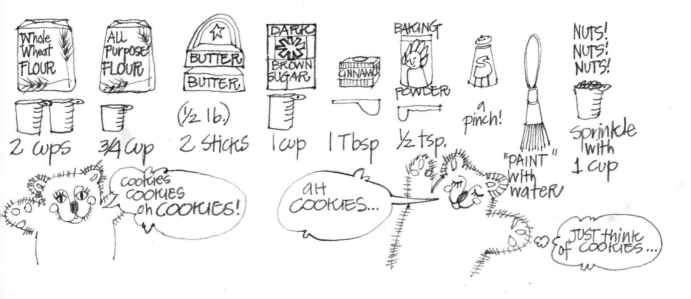

GINGERBREAD PEOPLE

You don't need a cookie cutter to make these gingerbread boys or girls.
You just shape them with your hands — as big or as small as you like.
This recipe will make a dozen fairly large people (about 8 inches tall)
or more smaller cookies.

Dancin' Gingerbreads

Some of the nicest people you know are gingerbread people. They come in many shapes & sizes but all one Beautiful Color.

La Cucaracha La Cucaracha

la la la la

Preheat the oven to 350°.

Pour **1 cup MOLASSES** into a small pan.

Heat it on the stove till it bubbles around the edge.

Meanwhile, butter 2 or 3 cookie sheets.

Pour the hot molasses into a large mixing bowl.

Cut up into little pieces **6 TABLESPOONS BUTTER.**

Put the butter into the hot molasses and stir it around till it's all melted. Then add:

> **2 tablespoons WATER**
> **½ cup BROWN SUGAR**
> **1 teaspoon CINNAMON**
> **½ teaspoon NUTMEG**
> **½ teaspoon CLOVES**
> **1 teaspoon GINGER**
> **½ teaspoon SALT**
> **½ teaspoon BAKING SODA**

Stir until all the dry things are dissolved. Then add:

> **3 cups WHOLE-WHEAT FLOUR**
> **½ cup POWDERED MILK**

Stir until it's all mixed together into a good dough. Add a bit more **FLOUR** if it's too sticky.

Now take a bowl of water. Dip your hands in the water so the dough doesn't stick to you. Shape the gingerbread people like this: Roll a small ball for the head and a larger ball for the body, 2 little snakes for arms and 2 bigger snakes for legs. Put them all together on the cookie sheet to make a person, and pat them out flat. (Of course you can also make other things besides people — animals, houses, cars, etc.)

Decorate your cookies with **RAISINS.**

Bake them about 5 minutes, till they're turning darker brown around the edges. Let them cool a minute or two on the cookie sheets, then take them off with a spatula to finish cooling.

POP TOP RAISIN BREAD

These loaves of bread come out round, because you bake them in coffee cans. The dough lets you know when it's ready to go in the oven by popping its top.

Measure into a large bowl:

½ cup WARM WATER
¼ teaspoon GINGER
1 teaspoon CINNAMON
½ teaspoon NUTMEG
1 tablespoon HONEY
2 packages YEAST

Let the bowl sit in a warm place for about 15 minutes, until the mixture is bubbly. (A good place is an oven with a pilot light, or over another bowl of warm water.)

Meanwhile, butter the insides of 2 one-pound coffee cans. Also, butter the plastic lids.

When the yeast mixture is bubbly, stir in:

3 tablespoons HONEY
1 teaspoon SALT
2 tablespoons SALAD OIL
1 large can (13 ounces) EVAPORATED MILK

Measure **4 cups UNBLEACHED FLOUR.**

Add the flour to the liquid mixture a little at a time, stirring it up well. The dough will be heavy and sticky. Then stir in:

1 cup WHEAT GERM
1 cup RAISINS

Put half the dough in each coffee can, and put the lids on. Put them in a warm place to rise, for about an hour, until the tops pop off.

Set the oven at 350°. Take the lids off the cans and bake the bread for about 45 minutes, until it is golden brown.

Let the bread cool in the cans for 5 or 10 minutes, then slide it out to cool some more.

POP TOP RAISIN BREAD

@ MEASURE INTO A BIG BOWL:

WARM

½ cup + ¼ tsp. + 1 tsp. + ½ tsp + 1 Tbsp. + 2 pckgs.

(GINGER) (CINNAMON) (NUT MEG) (HONEY) (YEAST)

◌ LEAVE BOWL to SIT
   IN WARM PLACE.
◌ Butter insides of
   2 cans & lids
◌ When yeast mix
   is bubbly STIR IN: 3 Tbsp + 1 tsp. + 2 Tbsp + large can

(HONEY)   (S)   (OIL)   EVAPORATED MILK 13 OZ

◌ Measure and add:

(FLOUR)   STIR IN: (WHEAT GERM) + (Raisins)

RAL can   RAL can   BREAD can   POP BREAD can   BREAD can

FRIED COOKIES

If you want to make cookies, but you don't have an oven, try these. In fact, try them sometime for a change even if you do have an oven, because they are good.

First, mix together in a big bowl:

3 tablespoons soft BUTTER
½ cup BROWN SUGAR

When the sugar is all mixed into the butter, sift into the bowl:

1 cup UNBLEACHED WHITE FLOUR
2 tablespoons POWDERED MILK
1 teaspoon BAKING POWDER
1 teaspoon CINNAMON
¼ teaspoon SALT

Then add: **½ cup WHEAT GERM**
1 EGG
3 tablespoons HONEY
½ cup RAISINS or CURRANTS

Mix this together with your hands until it makes a good dough.

Sprinkle some **FLOUR** around on a clean tabletop. Get some of the flour on your hands so the dough doesn't stick to them. Then shape pieces of the dough into little balls. Roll the balls around in the flour on the table, then flatten them out.

Heat an electric skillet to 300° and melt **1 tablespoon BUTTER** in it. (You can use a frying pan on the stove if you have to, but an electric skillet works the best.)

Put as many cookies as you can fit in the frying pan. Cook them until they start to puff up and are golden brown on the bottom. (This will take about 5 minutes.) Then turn them over with a spatula and cook for a minute or two on the other side. Take them out of the pan and let them cool.

Before you put more cookies in the pan to fry, put in more **BUTTER** and let it melt.

1 MIX

Butter
3 Tbsp.

+ ½ Cup

BROWN SUGAR

in a

GREAT BOWL

STOP. Go Sift ↑

2 SIFT

FLOUR
1 cup

Powdered MILK
+ 2 Tbsp +

1 tsp Baking Powder

+ CINNAMON 1 tsp. + ¼ tsp.

3 THEN ADD:

WHEAT GERM ½ Cup + 1 egg

+ 3 Tbsp Honey + ½ cup Raisins

really quick getaway.

oh rapture
oh cookies...

Runaway Cookie

4

• Shape balls
• FLATTEN •

300

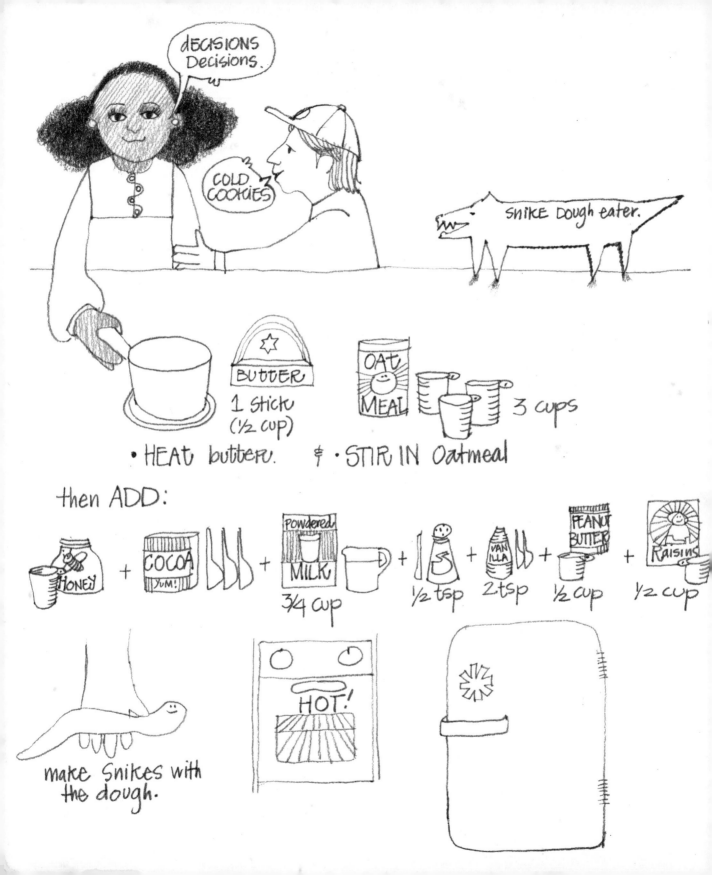

TWO-WAY COOKIES

After you've mixed up the dough, you can either bake these cookies in the oven or eat them unbaked. It's interesting to fix half the dough one way and half the other way, and see how they're different.

Put in a large pan **1 stick (½ cup) BUTTER or MARGARINE.**

Put it on top of the stove over low heat until the butter melts. Then stir in **3 cups OATMEAL (or OATMEAL mixed with WHEAT GERM).**

When the oatmeal and butter are well mixed, add:

> **1 cup HONEY**
> **3 tablespoons COCOA POWDER (unsweetened)**
> **¾ cup POWDERED MILK**
> **½ teaspoon SALT**
> **2 teaspoons VANILLA**
> **½ cup PEANUT BUTTER**
> **½ cup RAISINS**

Mix it well with your hands. It will be very stiff.

Then wash all the sticky dough off your hands. Put a bowl of water on the table and use it to wet your hands before you shape the cookies. This keeps the dough from sticking to you.

Roll the dough into little balls, or snakes, or any other shapes you can think of. Now you can either:

1 — Put the cookies on a lightly buttered cookie sheet, flatten them, and bake for 10 or 12 minutes in a 350° oven.

OR

2 — Eat the cookies right away. They'll be a little mushy, and if you want them harder, put them in the refrigerator for a while.

CHEESY TARTS

Preheat the oven to 350°.

Sift together into a big bowl:

> **2 cups FLOUR (whole-wheat or unbleached)**
> **1 teaspoon SALT**
> **¼ teaspoon BAKING POWDER**

Cut up into little pieces **1 stick COLD BUTTER.**
Rub the butter into the flour with your fingers until it's all crumbly.

In another bowl mix up:

> **1 cup COTTAGE CHEESE**
> **2 tablespoons HONEY**

Add this to the flour and butter mixture. Use your hands and mix it all up to a nice smooth dough.

Sprinkle a little more **FLOUR** around on a clean tabletop or pastry board. Then sprinkle some flour on the dough and roll it out with a rolling pin until it's as thin as a pie crust.

Cut the dough into any shapes you like and put the pieces on cookie sheets. (Or cut circles and press them into little tart pans if you have any.)

Spread a little **JAM** (any flavor you like) in the middle of each one.

Bake the tarts about 20 minutes. Let them cool for a few minutes before you eat them.

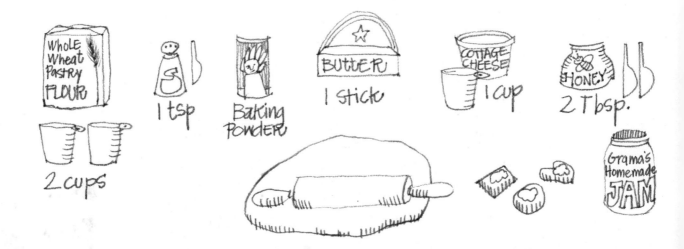

CHEESY FROSTING

Let one large (8-ounce) package of **CREAM CHEESE** sit in a bowl until it's soft. Mix in ¼ **cup COCOA POWDER** (unsweetened), if you want chocolate. If not, leave it out.

Add **1 teaspoon VANILLA.**

Then stir in **HONEY** until it tastes sweet enough (about 2 tablespoons).

Add a little **POWDERED MILK** (the non-instant, non-grainy kind is best) until just the right thickness.

Then spread it on your cake or cupcakes.

In hot weather you must refrigerate this, or it will get too soft.

MUD PIE CAKE

You don't even need a mixing bowl for this cake. Everything goes right into the pan. You can either bake it in the oven, or cook it in an electric skillet.

If you bake it, use a pan about 10 by 13 inches. Preheat the oven to 350°.

Don't grease the pan (or skillet). Sift into it:

> **2 cups WHOLE-WHEAT PASTRY FLOUR***
> **4 tablespoons COCOA POWDER (unsweetened)**
> **2 teaspoons BAKING SODA**
> **½ teaspoon SALT**

Poke three holes in the flour mixture. Pour into a two-cup measure:

> **½ cup VEGETABLE OIL**
> **1 cup HONEY**

Pour part of this mixture into each hole. Then put into the measuring cup:

> **1 cup COLD WATER**
> **2 tablespoons VINEGAR**
> **1 tablespoon VANILLA**

Pour this over the mixture in the pan. Then stir it all up with a slotted spatula, scraping up the bottom as you mix. All the dry and wet things should be pretty well mixed up, but it's okay for a few small lumps to be in the batter.

Bake the cake for 30 to 35 minutes. Or, if you're using an electric skillet, plug it in, put the cover on with the vent open, and set it at 250°. Cook it for 30 to 35 minutes. Either way, it's done when a toothpick stuck in the middle comes out with no batter on it.

Serve the cake from the pan, after it has cooled.

*If you don't have the pastry flour, substitute half regular whole-wheat and half unbleached white flour.

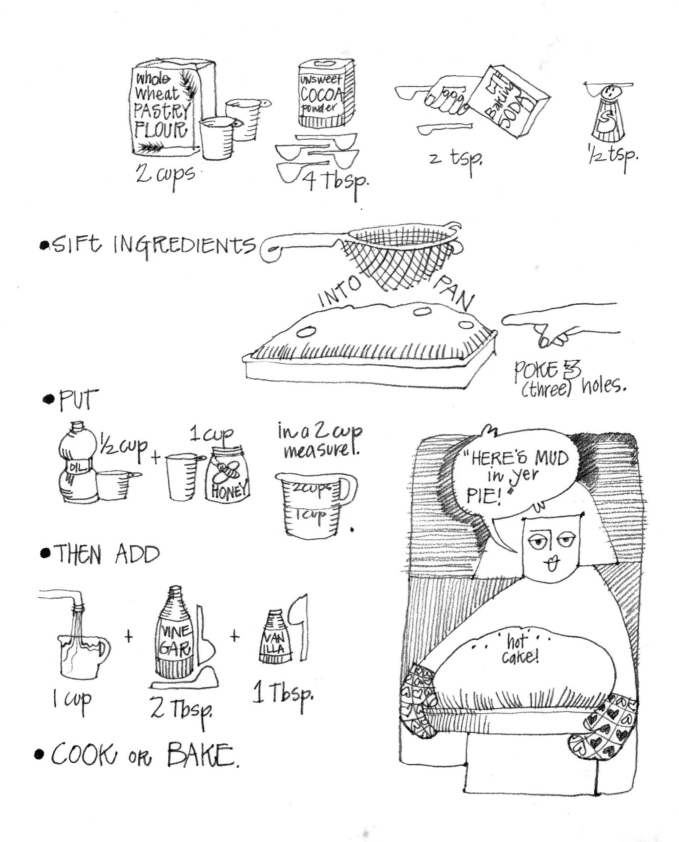

POOR MAN'S CAKE

This cake gets its name because you don't need eggs, milk, butter, or other expensive ingredients to make it. If you're feeling really poor, you can substitute water for the orange juice and use leftover bacon grease for the shortening, since the spices will hide the taste.

Another story about this cake is that it was traditionally made in Greece as an offering to the saint of the lost and found. When a person got back something he had lost, he showed his thanks by taking a cake like this to church to give to the poor.

Preheat the oven to 350°.

Put in a pan and boil for 5 minutes:

> **1 cup ORANGE JUICE**
> **½ cup SHORTENING**
> **1 cup RAISINS (or other chopped dried fruit)**
> **½ cup SUGAR**
> **½ cup HONEY (or CORN SYRUP)**
> **1 tablespoon CINNAMON (or mixed spices)**

Then put the pan in a slightly larger pan of ice water and beat it till it's cooled. (If you're not in a hurry, you can just put it in a cold place for an hour or so.)

Sift in: **2 cups FLOUR (whole-wheat or unbleached)**
        2 teaspoons BAKING POWDER
        ½ teaspoon BAKING SODA

Stir very well. Then grease an 8-inch loaf pan (or a 7-inch tube pan) and pour the batter into it.

You can sprinkle on ½ **cup SESAME SEEDS** if you like.

Bake it about 45 minutes, and let it cool in the pan.

CREAMY FROSTING

If you use plain whipping cream to frost a cake, it quickly gets soft and runny. But if you add a little gelatin, the icing stays nice and fluffy.

First, put **1 teaspoon GELATIN** (the plain, unsweetened kind) in a small pan with **1 tablespoon COLD WATER.** Put the pan on the stove over medium heat and stir it around until the gelatin is all dissolved.

Pour **1 cup HEAVY CREAM** into a bowl. Beat it with an egg beater until it is thick and fluffy.

Scrape the gelatin into the whipped cream, and add
3 tablespoons HONEY
1 teaspoon VANILLA.

Keep beating just until these things are mixed in.

Then frost your cake. If you don't eat it right away, keep it cool.

CLOUD FROSTING OF THE ANGELS.

GELATIN

COLD

½ PINT HEAVY CREAM

HONEY

VANILLA

FLUFFY cumulus cloud FROSTED CAKE.

FRUIT CANDIES

You will need about one cup each of three or four different kinds of dried fruit, such as:

**RAISINS
APRICOTS
DATES
PRUNES**

Make sure these are all pitted — that they don't have any seeds. Put them through a food grinder together with:

**½ cup NUTS (any kind you like)
the RIND of one ORANGE (washed)**

(To get the rind, you shave off the thin orange part on the outside with a vegetable peeler.)

Put all these ground-up things in a big bowl, along with **1 teaspoon ground GINGER.**

Mix it all up well. Then shape the mixture into little balls.

Roll the candies in grated **COCONUT** — either fresh or packaged.

Or, melt one small package of **CHOCOLATE CHIPS** over very low heat, adding a spoonful or two of water. Dip the candies in the melted chocolate till they are well covered. Put them on waxed paper to cool until the chocolate hardens.

Keep the candies in the refrigerator. Makes about 4 dozen.

COOKING FOR THE ANIMALS

The birds have a hard time finding food in the winter, when the ground is covered with snow and nothing is growing. So it's a good time to think of ways we can help them.

MAKING BIRD PUDDING

Mix up a nice yukky mess of:
> ½ pound LARD
> 1 cup PEANUT BUTTER
> OATMEAL — as much as you can add without
> making the pudding too dry

Collect **PINE CONES** and stick them in the pudding. Get as much pudding as you can on the ends of the pine cones, and hang them from a tree.

A CHRISTMAS TREE FOR THE BIRDS

You can make this by decorating a shrub in your yard (or even your discarded Christmas tree) with any or all of the following, which should attract a variety of birds.

> **PINE CONES with BIRD PUDDING**
> **A stale DONUT**
> **A "head" of SUNFLOWER SEEDS**
> **Sprigs of BERRIES**
> **Sliced ORANGES or GRAPEFRUITS**
> **Chunks of SUET**
> **Sprigs of MULTIFLORA ROSE HIPS**
> **Halves of COCONUTS**

PEANUT BUTTER LURE

This is a good way to discover what animals are living in your neighborhood. Try it when winter is ending and animals are coming out of hibernation to search for food.

Take a piece of **HEAVY CARDBOARD** and spread it with **PEANUT BUTTER.**

Leave it on the ground outside overnight. In the morning, see if there are any signs that animals were eating it. Look for tracks in the peanut butter. The Audubon Society puts out a little sheet showing many animal tracks to help with identification.

GRAHAM CRACKER CAKES

Instead of flour, these cupcakes are made with graham cracker crumbs. So the first thing to do is to crush up graham crackers until you have **2 cups GRAHAM CRACKER CRUMBS.**

This will take about half of a one-pound box of graham crackers. If several people are working together, you can divide up the crackers into several small paper bags. (Paper is better than plastic; it doesn't get holes in it so easily.) Let each person crush his own crackers any way he wants — pounding, squeezing, pressing, rolling with a rolling pin. The crackers should be as well mashed up as you can get them, but a few lumps are okay.

Heat the oven to 350°.

Next, melt in a large pan over low heat
> **½ cup BUTTER, MARGARINE, or SHORTENING**

Stir in
> **½ cup HONEY**
> **2 EGGS**

Beat this mixture with a wire whisk or egg beater for a couple of minutes.

In another pan or bowl mix the two cups of cracker crumbs together with
> **1½ teaspoons BAKING POWDER**
> **½ teaspoon BAKING SODA**
> **¼ teaspoon SALT**

Pour half the cracker mixture into the honey mixture. Stir well, then add **½ cup MILK.**

Stir again, then add the rest of the crumbs. Mix well.

Either grease cupcake pans or use paper liners — enough for 15 cupcakes. (Or you can make two 8-inch layers or one 9-inch square cake.) Fill the pans a little more than halfway. Bake about 20 minutes.

SPRING!

SPRING

Spring is a time for the sap to flow. We tap a nearby maple tree and boil down our own syrup to serve with pancakes.

Spring is time for eggs to hatch. We cook scrambled eggs and color the shells.

Spring is a time for planting. We plant our own seeds indoors in early spring.

We visit a farm, where we see the planting begin. We see the animals who give us eggs and milk, and we think of other ways to use these things.

Spring is a time of growing, and we think of different ways that things can grow. We bake bread, and watch the yeast grow to make it rise. We make yogurt, and watch the culture grow to make it thicken.

Spring is a time for gathering new plants and seeing what we can observe and learn about them.

Spring is a good time for testing new skills. From all we have learned, we make up our own recipes.

PANCAKES and SYRUP

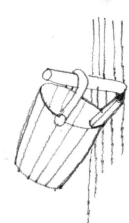

One spring the children and teachers at our school tapped a nearby parent's maple tree. (To do this, we drilled a hole into the trunk. Then we put a spout in the hole and hung a bucket on the spout. We collected the sap for several days and brought it back to school.) When we had several gallons of sap we boiled it slowly for several days until we got maple syrup.

We found out that it takes a **lot** of sap to get a little syrup. We had to go to the store for more syrup to have enough to go around.

To go with the delicious syrup, we made some pancakes. We started by grinding several kinds of grain — wheat, corn, oats — into flour. We mixed this with some white flour for a smoother texture.

We put the flour on a table with the rest of the ingredients. Each child had a paper juice cup and measured the ingredients for his/her own pancake. In each cup we put:

> **1 EGG**
> **4 tablespoons FLOUR**
> **½ teaspoon BAKING POWDER**
> **2 tablespoons POWDERED MILK**
> **1 tablespoon CORN OIL**

Then we filled the cup almost to the top with **WATER** and stirred it up. Each person then cooked his own pancake in an electric frying pan, lightly oiled.

DAVID EYRE'S PANCAKE

We don't know who David Eyre is, but his pancake is delicious. It's different from most pancakes, because you cook it in the oven, not on top of the stove.

Preheat the oven to 425°.

Take a big (10- to 12-inch) skillet or other round pan that can go in the oven. Put in it **4 tablespoons BUTTER,** cut up in pieces. Put the pan in the oven until the butter melts.

Meanwhile, put in a bowl:

> **½ cup FLOUR (whole-wheat or unbleached)**
> **a pinch of CINNAMON**
> **½ cup MILK**
> **2 EGGS**

Stir them up until the flour is mixed in, but leave some lumps in the batter.

If you want, you can stir in some **FRUIT,** such as blueberries or chopped apples.

When the butter has melted, carefully take the pan out of the oven and pour in the batter. Put it back in the oven and bake 15 or 20 minutes until it is golden brown.

Take it out again, and sprinkle on **3 teaspoons SUGAR.**

Put it back in the oven one more time, for about 5 minutes.

Meanwhile, squeeze the **JUICE out of one LEMON.** Take the pancake out of the oven, and pour the juice over the top.

Cut it into wedges and serve at once. Makes a good breakfast for 4 people.

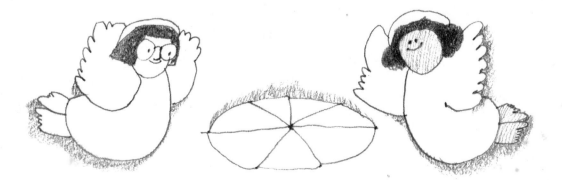

DUTCH PANCAKES

The parent who taught us how to make these very special pancakes wrote: "In Holland my mother (and all other mothers I knew) would never measure their ingredients for this recipe. They would start out with a certain amount of flour estimated by eye. Then they would crack one egg on top of the flour, add milk and mix with a wooden spoon till all lumps were gone and the right consistency was reached, adding a little salt to taste. The more milk is added, the thinner the pancakes."

We made these for lunch at school one day after we had gone blueberry picking, so we cooked blueberries into them. But you can experiment with using any kind of fresh or dried fruits, or chopped nuts, in any combinations you like. It's fun to have bowls of several different kinds of fruits and nuts and let each person sprinkle what he/she wants on his/her own pancake.

First, make the batter. (These amounts will serve 6 to 8 people.)

Put in a big bowl: **2 cups UNBLEACHED FLOUR.** With a wooden spoon poke a hole in the flour and pour into it

> **1 EGG**
> **2 cups MILK**
> **½ teaspoon SALT**

Beat it well until all the lumps are gone. In Holland they use a special wooden spoon with a hole in the middle. But you can use a regular wooden spoon, or an egg beater, or a wire whisk. Gradually add more **MILK — ½ cup,** or a little more to make a rather thin batter.

Cook the pancakes in a round skillet on the stove or in an electric skillet. You must get the pan quite hot before you pour in the batter, or the pancake will stick.

For each pancake you need about one strip of **BACON.** (If you don't have bacon you can coat the pan with salad oil, but bacon is tastier.)

Cut the bacon into three or four pieces. Cook these in the pan until they are almost brown.

Then dip out about ¼ cup of pancake batter. Pour it into the pan and tilt the pan around till the bottom is covered. (If your pan is very large, don't try to cover the whole pan.)

Sprinkle on whatever **FRUITS AND NUTS** you want. (Some suggestions: berries, chopped apples, raisins, sliced bananas, grated coconut, sesame or sunflower seeds, or anything else that sounds good.) Press them down into the pancake with a spatula. Cook it a few minutes, till the top is dry. Then flip it over (this is best done by an adult) and brown the other side.

Slide the pancake out onto a plate. Spread on syrup, honey, or jam. Roll it up and cut it into pieces to eat.

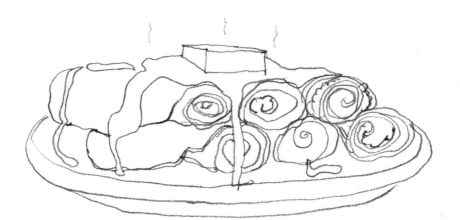

SCRAMBLED EGGS

You might get inspired to cook these after you've read Dr. Seuss's book, **Scrambled Eggs Super.**

For every person who wants to eat them, you should have **1 or 2 EGGS.**

The first thing to do, of course, is to get the eggs out of the shells. The easy way to do this is just to break them open. But you can also blow the egg out and be left with a whole shell, which is especially nice if you want to make Easter eggs. To blow the eggs, tap a little hole in each end of the shell. Use pointed scissors and make one hole a little bigger than the other. Be sure you poke through the skin inside the shell. Then blow hard into the small hole and the egg will come out the other hole. Rinse the shells out with water if you want to save them. You can paint them with poster paint and use them to make an egg tree.

If several people are cooking eggs, each one should have his own bowl or paper cup to put his egg into.

Pour a spoonful or so of **MILK** in with the egg.

Sprinkle on a little **SALT** and stir it all up.

Now add some **STUFF** — which can be almost anything. Some ideas are:

    CHEESE — any kind, cut up or grated, or cottage cheese
    MEAT — such as ham or chicken, cut into little pieces
    VEGETABLES — onions, carrots, tomatoes, peppers, or cooked
                        leftover vegetables, cut up
    SPROUTS — bean, wheat, alfalfa, etc.
    HERBS AND SPICES — basil, parsley, oregano, paprika, or
                        whatever
    ANYTHING ELSE you can think of, such as sesame seeds,
                  ketchup, etc., etc., etc.

Each person can make his own combination of "stuff." Two or three different things are usually enough.

Melt a little **BUTTER** in a frying pan and cook the eggs, one batch at a time, over medium low heat, stirring until they are solid but still soft.

FRESH BUTTER

You can make butter by beating up cream with an egg beater. But it's more fun to make your own butter churn. What you need are:

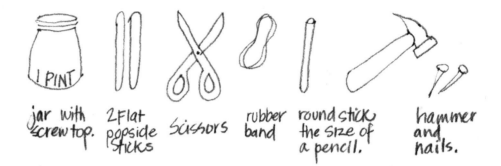

jar with screw top. 2 Flat popside sticks scissors rubber band round stick the size of a pencil. hammer and nails.

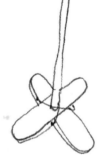

A one-pint jar with screw top, 2 flat popsicle sticks, scissors, a rubber band, a round stick about the size of a pencil, hammer and nails.

First, make the dasher. Cut the popsicle sticks so that they just fit into the bottom of the jar, lying flat. Fasten them together with a rubber band, into an X shape. Hammer a small nail through the center of the popsicle sticks into the bottom of the long stick, so the X has a handle sticking straight up.

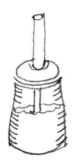

Next, take a large nail (or a pointed screwdriver) and hammer a hole in the top of the jar, big enough for the stick to go through. Pull the nail out.

Pour into the jar ½ **pint HEAVY CREAM.**

Put the dasher in the jar and tightly screw on the top so that the stick comes through the hole.

Now you're ready to churn — move the dasher up and down very fast. After a while the cream will get very thick, and you will have whipped cream. Keep on churning, and soon lumps of butter will appear. The lumps will get bigger and bigger until all the butter is separated out. (The liquid left in the jar is **buttermilk.**)

Put the butter in a bowl and pour a little **ICE WATER** on it. Press the water through the butter with a wooden spoon. The water will turn white, as the rest of the milk separates out from the butter. Pour off the liquid.

Mix a little **SALT** into the butter. Spread it on a piece of bread and eat it.

CHAPPATIS (Indian Fried Bread)

This is good to make with a group, because each person can shape and cook his own.

Put into a large bowl:

2 cups WHOLE-WHEAT FLOUR
2 cups UNBLEACHED WHITE FLOUR
1 teaspoon SALT
3 tablespoons OIL or MELTED BUTTER
WATER, enough to make a soft dough

Mix together and knead a lot — five or ten minutes. You can break the dough into small balls so everyone will have one to knead.

Put all the dough back in the bowl, cover with a damp cloth, and let it sit for 45 minutes to 1 hour.

Shape the dough into balls the size of a big marble (makes about 50) and roll or pat them flat.

Melt a pat of **BUTTER** in a frying pan over medium heat. Fry a few pieces of dough at a time, adding more butter as you need it.

Serve the bread warm with butter and jelly.

YOGURT

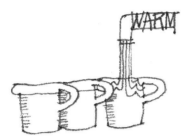

One way of making yogurt is to heat some milk to the right temperature (about 110°), stir in a spoonful of already-made yogurt, and let it sit in a warm place for several hours. Here's a recipe that uses powdered and evaporated milk, and doesn't need a stove or thermometer. It makes a quart of yogurt, for less than half the cost of store-bought.

Measure **3 cups WARM WATER.**

It should feel just nice and warm on your wrist — not too hot and not cool. Put it in a bottle or jar with a tight-fitting lid, one-quart size or larger.

Measure **1½ cups INSTANT POWDERED MILK** (see note below).

Stir the dry milk into the water, screw the top tightly on the jar, and shake it up very well so that there are no lumps. (Or you can mix this in an electric blender.)

Add **1 small can EVAPORATED MILK** (5⅓ ounces)
    1½ tablespoons YOGURT

Stir this well and pour into one or more glass or plastic jars with covers. They should have a wide enough opening so that the finished yogurt can be easily spooned out. Put the tops on the jars.

Set the jars in a pot that is as high or higher than they are. Put hot water in the pot until it comes almost to the top of the jars. The water should feel a little hotter than the warm water you started with, but not hot enough to burn.

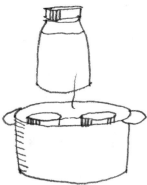

Now all you have to do is keep it warm — but not hot — for at least 4 hours. You can just wrap the pot in heavy towels or blankets. Or put it in an oven with a pilot light. You can also use a covered picnic cooler or ice bucket filled with hot water. Or you can pour the yogurt into a thermos.

Don't bother it for at least 4 hours, because yogurt doesn't like to be shaken up while it is setting. After 4 to 6 hours it will have thickened, so that it jiggles instead of sloshes in the jar. The longer it sits after thickening, the tangier it will get.

Put it in the refrigerator for a few hours and it will be ready to eat. Don't eat it all, but save a few spoonfuls to start your next batch.

Note: Some people feel you get smoother yogurt from non-instant powdered milk (sold in health-food stores). We've found that the instant kind works perfectly well, and it is cheaper and easier to find. If you do use non-instant milk, decrease the amount to 1 cup powdered milk.

What can you do with YOGURT?

Make a Yogurt Sundae. Put some yogurt in a dish. Add fresh fruit. Pour on honey. Sprinkle on granola.

Make Yogurt Popsicles. Mix 1 quart **YOGURT** with 1 large can **FROZEN ORANGE JUICE.** Add 1 tablespoon **VANILLA,** ¼ cup **HONEY.** Freeze in popsicle molds or paper cups.

Make Frozen Yogurt. Mix yogurt with mashed fresh fruit. Sweeten to taste and freeze. Serve like ice cream. Guaranteed to please even people who hate yogurt.

Make Yogurt Cheese. Put yogurt in a colander lined with muslin or 3 layers of cheesecloth. Set in the sink overnight to drain and thicken into cheese.

Use in cooking instead of sour cream or buttermilk.

Make a foolproof Sourdough Starter. Mix 1 cup yogurt with 1 cup unbleached flour. Let sit at room temperature 3 to 5 days, till it's bubbly and smells sour; then refrigerate. Use in any sourdough recipe. (Replace starter used in cooking with equal parts milk and flour, and let sit overnight to sour.)

Add your own ideas here:

ORANGE CUPCAKES

These little cakes use yeast to make them rise, rather than baking powder.

Put into a medium-sized pan, and heat just until warm:

> **1 cup ORANGE JUICE**

Stir in: **1 package YEAST**
1 tablespoon HONEY

Sift in: **1 cup WHOLE-WHEAT FLOUR**

Let this sit in a warm place until bubbly, about 10 or 15 minutes.

Meanwhile, put into a mixing bowl:

> **1 EGG**

Beat the egg with an egg beater until it is foamy. Then stir in:

> **⅓ cup SALAD OIL**
> **⅔ cup HONEY**
> **1 cup sifted WHOLE-WHEAT FLOUR**
> **½ teaspoon SALT**
> **1 teaspoon VANILLA**

When the yeast mixture is bubbly, stir it into the egg mixture.

You will need enough muffin tins to make 18 cupcakes. (Or you can bake all or part of the batter in a loaf pan.) Either butter the muffin pans or use paper cupcake liners. Fill each space half full of batter.

Turn the oven to 150°. Let the cupcakes rise in the oven about 40 minutes, till they almost reach the top of the pan. Then turn the oven to 350° and bake them for 20 minutes.

If you want to frost them, let them cool first.

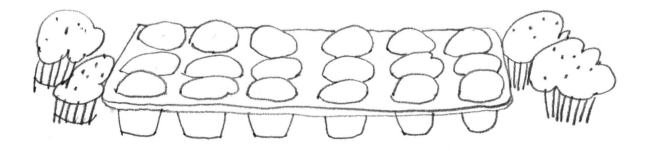

COOKS WITHOUT BOOKS

One day at Parents' Nursery School we decided to make up some recipes of our own. Here's what the teachers put out on the cooking table:

Unbleached white flour
Wheat berries to grind to whole-wheat flour
A dozen eggs
Powdered milk
Evaporated milk
Carob powder
Nuts — walnuts, almonds, pecans
A couple of potatoes
A couple of carrots
One coconut
Powdered sugar
Granulated white sugar
Brown sugar
Molasses
Baking powder
Margarine
Nutmeg
Apple juice
Water

We also had measuring cups and measuring spoons, mixing bowls and mixing spoons, and egg beaters.

Anybody who wanted to make up a recipe did all the measuring and mixing, and the teacher wrote down what went in. When the child was in doubt, he was encouraged to taste the ingredient in question before adding it.

The final products were sampled by children, teachers, and parents. On the next few pages are some of the most successful concoctions. Try them — **we** liked them!

JULIA'S COCONUT CAKE

Julia put a lot of different things in her recipe. Someone told her she was a really good maker, and she said, "I know, I might be a chef when I grow up."

To start with, she took a screwdriver and hammered it into a coconut to get the juice out. She used about:

    ¼ **cup COCONUT JUICE**

She put the coconut juice in a bowl and added:

    4 WALNUTS, shelled and ground
    1⅓ cups WHITE FLOUR
    2 EGGS
    1 teaspoon BAKING POWDER
    2 tablespoons CAROB POWDER
    3 tablespoons POWDERED SUGAR
    a sprinkle of GRANULATED SUGAR
    1½ cups GROUND COCONUT
    ½ stick MARGARINE
    1⅓ cups WHOLE-WHEAT FLOUR
    a little nutmeg
    EVAPORATED MILK to make a good batter

She mixed all these things up well. Then she buttered a pan, put the batter in it, and baked the cake in an oven set at 350° till it seemed done.

ALICE'S CHOCOLATE CAKE

Alice said, "This is going to be a regular cake, not a birthday cake."
Here's what she put in it:

- ¼ cup WHITE SUGAR
- ½ cup BROWN SUGAR
- 1 teaspoon MOLASSES
- 2 fat slices BUTTER (about ¼ cup)
- 1 cup WATER
- ½ cup APPLE JUICE
- 1½ cups WHITE FLOUR
- 1 heaping teaspoon BAKING POWDER
- ½ teaspoon SALT
- ¼ cup CAROB POWDER
- ¾ cup GROUND WHEAT BERRIES

She mixed this up well, then poured it into a buttered baking pan. Then
it went into the oven (set at about 350°) until it looked done.

CHRIS AND JODY'S NUT BREAD

Chris and Jody decided to make something together.
First, they shelled 4 nuts and ground them up:

1 ALMOND
1 PECAN
2 WALNUTS

They tasted the carob powder and decided it tasted "between sugar and spice."   So they put in:

1 tablespoon CAROB POWDER

Then they added:

1 cup WHITE FLOUR
2 EGGS
2 tablespoons POWDERED SUGAR
a sprinkle of WHITE SUGAR
WHOLE-WHEAT BERRIES, ground into ½ cup flour
2 chunks of COCONUT, ground up

When this was all stirred up together, they put it in a buttered pan and cooked it in the oven at about 350° till it was done.

Matthew's Recipe for Applesauce

Put a cup of sugar in and a flavor of applesauce and now put in some apples and then we put in, I think, a little bit of the color of applesauce, then you put it in a grinder and grind it all up and get juice and put it in a stove and cook it for a while and when the bell rings you go down and see if it's doing all right. And then cook it for a minute or two. When the next bell rings you go down and check it again.

Becca's Recipe for Milkshakes...

We put some milk in and some ice cream in a thing. You put colors of paint in and you put the cap on so it won't spill out and you shake it up really fast and for a long time. And you know how much tons of ice cream you put in? 500 tons.

...and Advice on Making a Cake

It should be a vanilla cake because Becca's allergic to chocolate. The frosting should be a little bit not sweet but a little bit sweet because you know children like sweets.

WHAT IS IT?

This was a guessing game, where several children tried to guess what the something was that the teacher put on the table. Here are the answers they came up with:

1. A real bent candy cane
2. A plant
3. A snail
4. A half-curled-up snake
5. A music go-round
6. A spiral
7. Leaves are coming out
8. A fern
9. A letter J
10. A decoration
11. A lollipop
12. A snail curled up with a little tail
13. Ferns are coming out of it
14. A tittle
15. A hook
16. A number 9
17. Hobby horses
18. A snail with green paint on top
19. A bean sprout
20. Yukky balls
21. A puppy — a hairy one

On the next page, you can see what it was, and what we did with it.

FIDDLEHEAD FERN

After we had finished the guessing game, we cooked the ferns and ate them. They were delicious.

Here's how to cook them:

Before the teacher brought these in, they had been soaked in water overnight.

After soaking them, you peel them to get all the fuzzy part off.

Then cook them in a little water until they're tender.

Add butter and salt, and eat.

SUMMER

Summer is a time for picnics.

Summer is a time for planting things outdoors.

Summer is a time for fresh fruits and vegetables, and making delicious salads.

Summer is a good time for milkshakes, for a quick meal on a hot day.

Summer is a good time for making cheese, which ripens quickly on hot days.

Summer is the best time for ice cream.

SUPERMILKSHAKE

This is good for a quick meal or snack. The exact measurements aren't too important. You can mix up any amounts that taste good.

Pour into a jar that holds one quart:

1 cup MILK
½ cup YOGURT
2 EGGS
1 small can FROZEN ORANGE JUICE
¼ cup POWDERED MILK (or MALTED MILK POWDER)
¼ cup COCOA POWDER (unsweetened)
¼ cup HONEY
1 teaspoon VANILLA

Shake this up very well. (You can also mix it in a blender.)

Then add enough **MILK** to fill the jar.

Drink as much as you want, and keep the rest in the refrigerator.

NOTE: Some people feel that raw eggs, especially raw egg whites, aren't good for you. You can leave the eggs out if you want (though they do supply a lot of protein), or just use the yolks. There doesn't seem to be any really strong proof that raw eggs are dangerous, but you should be careful not to use eggs that have gotten cracked in the box, because some germs might have gotten into them. Cracked eggs should always be cooked, to kill the germs.

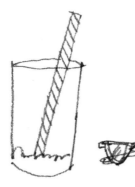

BERRY PUDDING

This is a Norwegian recipe, and in Norway it's called RODGRED MED FLODE.

Start by washing 3 pints of **STRAWBERRIES or RASPBERRIES.**

To wash them, you put them in a colander (a bowl with holes in it) and run water over them while you mix them up gently.

Then take off the little green tops and put the berries through a food mill.

Put the mashed-up berries in a pan and cook them, stirring, over medium high heat until they are boiling.

Take the pan off the heat.

Make a paste of: **¼ cup COLD WATER**
2 tablespoons ARROWROOT POWDER

Add this to the berry mixture and put the pan back on the stove, over low heat. Cook it until it is thick, but DO NOT let it boil again.

Let it cool a bit, then add a little **SUGAR or HONEY** until it tastes sweet enough.

Serve the pudding warm or chilled, plain, or with cream and slivered almonds.

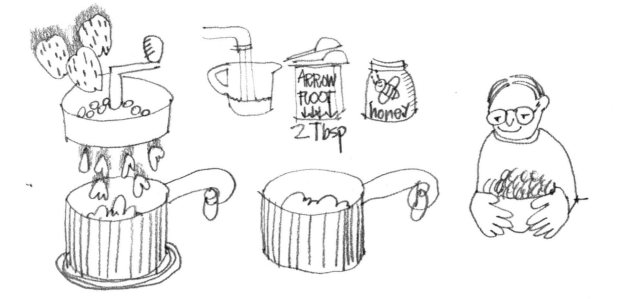

SALADS

Salads are good anytime, but they're especially good in summer. A cool salad tastes refreshing on a hot day, and in summer there are many fresh fruits and vegetables to choose from.

A good way of making salads in school is for each person to bring in one fruit or vegetable. Here are some ideas and questions you can think about when making salads.

Which are fruits and which are vegetables?

What different parts of the plants do they come from?

Are there any vegetables you should cook before putting in the salad? (Example: potatoes)

Which things need to be peeled?

Which things should we chop? grind? grate? leave whole?

What other things can we put in salads besides fruits and vegetables? (Some ideas: cheese, hard-boiled eggs, bacon, nuts, seeds, popcorn)

What happens to different kinds of fruits and vegetables when they are cut open?
  (Some ideas for experiments:
  Sprinkle different cut vegetables with salt, to see how the juices are extracted.
  Leave some apples, bananas, etc., exposed to air; mix others with citrus juices.)

How should we serve the salad? All in one bowl? Or each thing on a separate plate, and let each person mix his own?

What things can we mix to make dressings for our salads?

What happens when you pour vinegar into oil? What happens if you mix the vinegar with an egg, and then add oil?

Taste some lemon juice. Taste some honey. Mix them together and see what happens to the different tastes.

What can you do with VEGETABLES

Eat them raw with a dip (cheese, yogurt, sour cream, etc.).

Grind or grate them and cook in a frying pan with butter.

Mash cooked vegetables, mix with egg and cook like pancakes.

Make up combinations with other good things — like cheese, nuts, sesame seeds.

Mix hot vegetable cooking liquid with a little vinegar and use to color Easter eggs — red from beets, yellow from onion skins, green from spinach, etc., etc.

Add your own ideas here:

PITA (FLAT BREAD)

This bread from the Middle East is round and flat. It looks something like a pancake, but it's hollow, so you can cut each piece in half and stuff it with either a warm or cold filling for an instant sandwich.

Preheat the oven to 500°.

Measure into a large bowl 1¼ **cups LUKEWARM WATER**
        2 teaspoons HONEY

Stir in **1 package YEAST.** Let it sit in a warm place for about 5 minutes until it bubbles.

Stir in: **1 teaspoon SALT**
       3 cups FLOUR

(You can use either all unbleached flour, or half white flour and half whole-wheat.)

Knead the dough for about 10 minutes. If several people are working, let one knead all the dough for a few minutes. Then divide it up into several pieces and keep kneading. Sprinkle on a little more flour if it's too sticky.

Divide the dough into about 12 small balls. Roll or pat the balls flat. They'll be about 6 inches across and ¼ inch thick.

Put them on lightly buttered cookie sheets. Cover with a damp cloth and let them rise in a warm place for about 45 minutes. They'll puff up.

Bake the bread for 12 minutes until lightly browned.

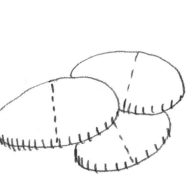

ENGLISH MUFFINS

You'll need to collect some empty tuna fish cans before you start to make these muffins. It's a good idea, if this is a group project, to have one can for each person.

Take the tops off the cans. Wash them and smear oil around the inside.

Start by scalding **1 cup MILK.**

Scalding means to heat the milk until it is very hot but not quite boiling. Stir in:

> **¼ cup MARGARINE**
> **1½ teaspoons SALT**
> **1 tablespoon CORN OIL**

Let this mixture cool just until it is lukewarm. A drop on your wrist will feel just in between cool and warm. Then stir in:

> **1 package YEAST**
> **3 cups FLOUR**

You can use either all unbleached white flour, or half white and half whole-wheat.

Knead the dough for about 5 or 10 minutes, until it is smooth.

Roll it out with a rolling pin, about ¼ inch thick. Cut out circles with the upside-down cans. Or pinch off balls of dough and pat them flat. Then put a circle of dough in each can and let it rise for an hour or so. You can see how much farther up the cans the dough has grown after an hour.

Take the muffins out of the cans and sprinkle them with **CORNMEAL.**

Cook them in a hot ungreased frying pan 7 minutes on one side. Then turn them over and cook 7 minutes on the other side.

We ate these for lunch one day at school with two kinds of salad, made from vegetables and fruits we had brought from home.

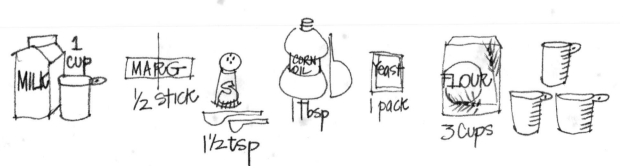

PRETZELS

Pretzels are a very old form of bread; they were first made at least two thousand years ago. These are the big, soft, chewy kind. They're very good eaten warm from the oven. But they also keep well, so you can make some extras to take along on picnics, for example.

This recipe calls for part rye flour, which adds a deliciously different taste. You could substitute whole-wheat flour for the rye. Plan on about 3 hours from start to finish. Makes about 18 big pretzels.

Measure **½ cup WARM WATER.** Pour it into a large mixing bowl and stir in **1 package YEAST.** Then stir in:

> **¼ cup HONEY**
> **1½ teaspoons SALT**
> **1 large can EVAPORATED MILK (13 ounces), plus enough WARM**
>   **WATER to make 2 cups**
> **¼ cup VEGETABLE OIL**

Pour in slowly: **1½ cups RYE FLOUR**
            1 cup UNBLEACHED WHITE FLOUR

Stir as you pour, until all the flour is well mixed in. Then cover the bowl and let dough rise in a warm place (such as over a bowl of warm water) for about 40 minutes, until it's bubbly.

Meanwhile, grease well 3 cookie sheets.

Sift together: **1½ cups UNBLEACHED FLOUR**
            ¾ teaspoon BAKING POWDER

Add it to the batter, along with **1½ cups RYE FLOUR.** Stir well till the flour is mixed in.

Sprinkle more flour (either kind) on a clean tabletop. Knead 5 minutes or longer, adding more flour as needed, until the dough is smooth and not sticky.

Break off pieces of dough and roll them out into long snakes. They should be about ½ inch thick and 20 inches long to make a regular-sized pretzel. Tie each one in a loose knot to form a pretzel shape (as shown), or make other shapes if you want. Put the shaped pretzels on the greased baking sheets and let them rise, uncovered, for 30 minutes in a warm place.

Meanwhile, preheat the oven to 400°.

Put **2 quarts WATER plus 3 tablespoons SALT** in a big pot and start it boiling. When the pretzels have risen, dip each one in boiling water for 2 seconds. (This gives them a nice shiny crust.)

A good way to do the dunking is to put the pretzels, one or two at a time, in a big wire strainer or French-fry basket. Have a big stack of paper towels nearby. Dip the strainer in the water, count to two, then set it out on the paper towels to drain for a second. Dump the pretzels out on the baking sheet. Continue till all the pretzels are done.

Take the **WHITE OF 1 EGG.** (You can separate it from the yolk by pouring the egg through your fingers.) Add **1 tablespoon WATER** and beat slightly with a fork. Using a pastry brush, paint the pretzels all over with the egg white. Sprinkle the pretzels with **COARSE KOSHER-TYPE SALT.**

Bake them for about 20 minutes until they are golden brown. Serve warm (with butter or mustard if you like), or wrap them well and keep for later. (You can reheat them if you want to.)

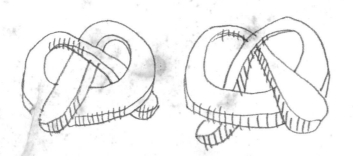

A GREAT CHEESE

CHEESE as easy as 1-2-3

Did you ever wonder what the curds and whey were that Little Miss Muffet was eating? Do you know how cheesecloth got its name? You can find out both these things by making your own cheese. It's very easy, because the milk does most of the work by itself.

The finished cheese is sort of a cross between cream cheese and cottage cheese, but has a rich, fresh taste unlike anything you can buy.

In the summer, when the days are warm, you can make the cheese in about three days. In cold weather it will take a bit longer.

2 quarts = 1 half gallon

MAKING CHEESE

BUTTER MILK

¼ CUP

First day. You can start with either milk or cream. Heavy cream will give the sweetest cheese, skim milk the sharpest taste, with light cream and whole milk in between. To get about one pint of cheese, begin with:

2 quarts WHOLE or SKIM MILK
(or 1 quart LIGHT CREAM)
(or 3 cups HEAVY CREAM)

Pour the milk or cream into a large pan. Put it on the stove over medium heat, and heat it just to lukewarm. (That's 90° to 100° if you have a thermometer, but you don't really need one. You can tell when it's right by dropping a bit on your wrist. It should not feel either cold or warm, but just the same temperature as your skin.)

Then stir in:

¼ cup BUTTERMILK, if you started with milk
(or 2 tablespoons BUTTERMILK, if you used cream)

Take the pan off the stove, cover it, and put it somewhere out of the way for a day, in a place not too cold or too hot.

Second day. Look at the milk mixture and see how it has changed. It should have gotten thick enough to look like soft yogurt or creamy jello. If it isn't quite that thick, leave it alone for a few more hours, or another day.

Next, you need a large colander (that's a bowl with holes in it) and a piece of cheesecloth. Cover the inside of the colander with two or three layers of the cheesecloth. Put the colander in the sink and pour the thickened milk into it. The thick part that stays in the colander is called the *curd*. The watery part that goes down the drain is called the *whey*.

Leave the colander in the sink for about 10 minutes. Then cover the top of the curd with cheesecloth, and cover the whole thing with some plastic wrap or foil. Put it where it can drain for a day, either on the sink or on a rack over a large pan.

Third day. The cheese should now be a fairly solid mass. Scrape it out into a bowl and mix in **1 teaspoon SALT.**

You can eat some now, but if you don't want it all, rinse out the cheese-cloth and put it back in the colander. Then pour out the whey that has drained into the pan and put the cheese back in the cloth-lined colander over the pan. From now on you should keep it in the refrigerator.

After one more day of draining, you can take the cheese out of the colander and keep it in a covered dish or wrap it in plastic wrap.

You can serve the cheese plain, spread on crackers or bread, or on raw vegetables like celery or carrots. Or you can make a really delicious dessert by mixing it with some **SWEETENED WHIPPED CREAM** and **VANILLA** and serving it with **FRESH FRUIT.**

ice cream

One of the best summer treats you can have is homemade ice cream. And you can make it even if you don't have an ice cream freezer. Here's how to put together your own ice cream machine — it won't cost a cent, it will make delicious ice cream (with a little muscle power), and it will let you see and feel exactly what's happening as the ice cream freezes.

All you need are an ice bucket or a plastic or wooden pail, plus a clean coffee can with a plastic lid. In a one-pound can you can make about a pint of ice cream.

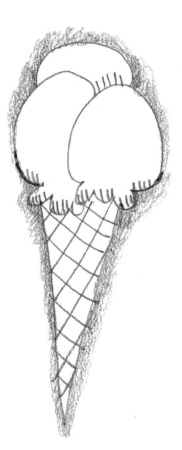

First, beat together in the coffee can

> **1 EGG**
> **¼ cup HONEY**

Add

> **1 cup MILK**
> **½ cup CREAM**
> **1 teaspoon VANILLA**
> **a dash of SALT**

You don't want to fill the can much more than halfway, or the ice cream will slop over the sides as you freeze it.

Put a layer of **ICE** in the bottom of the pail. Crushed ice freezes smoother and faster, but cubes will work perfectly well. (Or if you decide to make ice cream in winter you can use snow, instead of ice.) Sprinkle the ice with a spoonful of **SALT**. Rock salt, which you buy in a hardware store, works best, but you **can** use table salt.

Now put the plastic cover on the coffee can and set the can on top of the ice. Pack more salt and ice in the pail around the sides of the can. When the ice is almost to the top of the can, take off the plastic lid.

Stir the ice cream mixture around and around with a big spoon, letting the can turn, too. Keep on stirring and watching. You'll want several people to take turns, because it will take from 15 to 30 minutes for the cream to freeze to mush.

You'll probably want to eat it right away, while it's still soft. But if you want to wait while it hardens, put more ice and salt around the can, cover the whole thing, and let it sit for an hour or two. (Or just put the can in the refrigerator freezer.)

If you want to set up more than one freezer you could try some experiments. See what would happen if you tried to freeze one can of ice cream without stirring it. Or if you only used ice and no salt.

FRUIT LEATHER

If you find overripe or bruised fruit on sale, you can use it to make this delicious candy which will keep for months (though it tastes so good it probably won't stay around that long.) All you have to do is mash and strain the fruit, heat it for a few minutes, then let it dry in the sun or any warm place.

We made ours from peaches; you could also use apricots or strawberries. Apples also make a delicious leather, but you have to cook them into applesauce before you mash them.

First, cut up some ripe **PEACHES.** Take out the pits and put the peaches through a food mill (using the largest holes).

Put the peach pulp into a large pot and add **1 tablespoon HONEY** for each pound of fruit that you started with. Heat and stir the mixture until it boils; then cook it two or three minutes.

Let it cool while you prepare the drying surface.

For each pound of fruit you began with, you will need three paper plates. Cover each plate with plastic wrap stretched around and taped to the back of the plate so the plastic stays tight and flat. Pour enough peach mush on each plate just to cover the bottom in a thin layer.

For the best flavor, dry the fruit outdoors in the sun. Put the plates in shallow pans or boxes. Stretch cheesecloth over the boxes and fasten it to the sides, but don't let it touch the fruit. This keeps the bugs out while letting the sun through. Depending on how hot the sun is, the drying will take one or more days. Be sure to bring the fruit inside at night.

If the weather doesn't cooperate you can do the drying indoors in a gas oven with a pilot light, or an electric oven set on the lowest heat. In the oven, of course, there's no need for the cheesecloth.

Don't try outdoor drying in very humid weather, because if the fruit stays damp too long it will get moldy. If the weather turns bad, you can always finish the drying in the oven.

The fruit leather is ready when it no longer feels wet and you can peel it away from the plastic wrap. Tear it into pieces to eat, or roll it up and store it covered with plastic.

GUIDELINES FOR TEACHERS AND PARENTS

At Parents' Nursery School we discovered that children as young as three and four can cook. They can cut with sawtoothed knives, grind with food and grain grinders, crack nuts with hammers, break open eggs, pop corn in popcorn poppers, turn over pancakes, as well as stir, pour, mix, measure, beat, and squeeze.

It was hard to believe at first, but the proof was "Thanksgiving Soup," made by three- and four-year-olds, really made by the kids — they did all the cutting, scraping, scrubbing, and stirring — and served outside, hot and delicious, at the end of a chilly November morning, to everyone — kids, parents, brothers, sisters, friends, teachers, and passers-by. Seeing — in this case eating — is believing. It takes patience and faith and a giant step back from preconceived ideas of the "right" way to do things in the kitchen.

When we make soups, salads, or any mixtures we "brainstorm" — "What can we put into the pot?" When we make our lunch (once a week) we brainstorm, too — "What do we like to eat for lunch?" We encourage and accept as many ideas as we can get — wild suggestions as well as more conventional ones — without criticizing or pushing toward any predetermined answer. Children can and like to plan, and can be more experimental than adults. The solution is to relax, take a deep breath, and *try* some of their ideas. Tiny radish leaves in a salad were delicious, as were some of their more complicated recipes. (See the section of recipes, headed "Cooks without Books.")

Here are some possibilities for brainstorming in cooking:

How can we measure things? How else?

What else can we do with food?

What are the dangers?

How can we prevent accidents?

Where do we get the food? Where does it come from?

How can we get the ingredients?

What can we bring from home?

What foods are good for us?

Where do foods go after we eat them?

Where will the garbage go?

What can we name our concoctions?

How do we clean up and have fun doing it?

What can we do while waiting for the food to cook?

What do we need for trial recipes?

What to do next?

What *is* cooking? How and why do we do it? To begin with, we've found that for children, cooking is a form of *play* — they're fascinated by doing it, seeing changes, taking things apart, and putting them together to make something new, even when they're not interested in eating what they make. (But we did also discover that, generally, if they make it they eat it. Even lumpy pancakes made from flour they ground themselves were devoured eagerly, and nobody cared when our first batch of peanut butter was more like cornmeal than butter.)

We have tried to take the simple and familiar and expand it as far as possible — and as far as we can away from readymade products. Not all soup comes from cans, nor bread from packages, nor peanut butter from jars. When we can we like

to trace our ingredients right back to the earth —
growing tomatoes, pulling carrots, picking corn;
then by saving and planting some of the seeds,
starting the whole cycle over again. We also try
to follow a natural calendar, using seasonal foods
when possible. Our school animals are often in-
cluded, too (another part of the food chain), feast-
ing on peelings and parings or seeds and nuts.

Of course, the use of natural foods and unrefined
ingredients also has obvious nutritional benefits.
This aspect is perhaps of special interest to parents, who are more concerned with eating prob-
lems than the learning quotient of cooking. From
this standpoint we try to steer clear of gimmicks
(such as salads with bunny faces) while expanding
the cooking possibilities beyond the standard children's repertoire of candies and cookies. By em-
phasizing the process rather than the product,
children can have more fun making soup than
fudge. Still, as one little girl remarked, "You know,
children do like sweet things." So we have plenty
of sweet recipes, but their wholesome ingredients
provide more than empty calories.

There is a tremendous amount of learning involved
in cooking besides the fun and the eating. The
outline accompanying the recipe for "My Teacher's
Wedding Cake" is an example of this, based on
what actually happened when we made that recipe. Cooking, moreover, is an especially effective
technique for working with the child with learning
disabilities. The task of following directions given
orally or through reading with a prescribed se-
quence of steps is important for the child who
often jumbles the proper order of letters in a word
and/or facts in a story. Cooking requires good
eye-hand coordination in using the utensils for

mixing, pouring, slicing, chopping, peeling, etc., which can be geared to the child's abilities to assure *him* success and yet give him practice at the same time. The adventure of seeing, feeling, tasting, and smelling makes use of his senses in a very real way, giving him the kind of feedback that words cannot. He not only learns the characteristics of the food ingredients, but he begins to understand the numbers and fractions system from actually measuring the quantities. He learns definitions of words like sifting and grating by doing them himself. For the distractible child there are concrete directions to follow which help to hold his attention, plus the incentive of a delicious treat at the end to help him follow through.

Cooking in school, like any other activity, is a cumulative process, starting in a very simple way (which may not seem like "cooking" at all — cutting up and comparing apples, tomatoes, squashes, etc. — but is a step toward it) and gradually going on to the more complex. Some recipes evolve naturally out of this (see carrot salad as an example); that is, are "evented" by the children. For more standard or specific recipes we've found it a good idea to make a large simple poster, giving ingredients and directions with simple illustrations, such as are found in this book. (Older children can do this themselves.) Posted on the wall, this is much easier for young children to follow than a page from a book, and can also be a good introductory reading experience.

We cook often and in small groups, the type and amount of participation up to each child, but all equally recognized as part of the process. Some may prepare, some clean up, some walk to the store for ingredients, etc., and all activities are shared by boys and girls.

It doesn't take a lot of fancy equipment or a "real" kitchen to cook. We started with a handful of knives and wooden spoons, a grinder or two, a couple of battered pots, one hotplate, and one outlet. We did a *lot* of cooking with just that. Gradually parents and friends, impressed with these young cooks, donated or loaned much more — old waffle irons, an electric skillet, a small portable oven, even a small refrigerator. But there has also been a lot of improvisation — old tin boxes into cooky sheets, plastic pails into mixing bowls, etc. Here is a list of things we've found fun and useful to have. They've all been donated, loaned, or come cheaply from rummage sales, church and school fairs, etc.

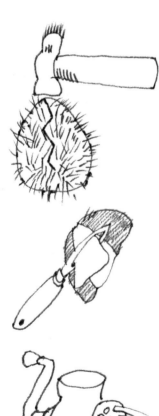

From the whole to the part:
Mashers
Saw-toothed steak knives
Hammers
Squeezers
Presses
Food mills
Grinders
Graters
Strainers
Vegetable peelers

Special purpose items:
Ice cream freezer
Popcorn popper
Noodle maker
Vegetable steamer

Stirrers:
Spatulas
Beaters

Wooden spoons
Wire whisks
Rolling pins
Containers:
Bowls (all kinds and sizes)
Pie and cake tins
Muffin pans
Ice cube trays
Coffee cans
Paper bags, paper cups

Safety is a very important aspect of cooking, and we have found that it can be directly related to what we consider another very worthwhile aspect — parent participation. It works both ways — parents enjoy helping, or even just watching, and the extra adults insure safety (as well as some exciting cooking experiences if a parent brings along his or her ice cream freezer, noodle maker, or whatever). Some of the tips for safety we have evolved are outlined here:

1. Anticipate the points of trouble (i.e., think through the whole cooking process before you start).

2. Prepare ahead of time a work area *at the child's level.*

3. Have a specific place for utensils to which they can be quickly returned, appropriately within or outside of (as for sharp knives) the reach of the children.

4. Maintain strict supervision around heat, with no child-level burner or appliance left unguarded (those extra parents are very welcome here).

5. Cut in half fruits and vegetables that might slip or roll when chopped.

6. Have a large low table or floor space for hammering nuts — and no more than a couple of hammers available at once.

7. Use semi-sharp knives, with serrated edges (old, used steak knives are good).

8. Keep the size of the cooking group small (usually about five or six involved in any one step). Have enough other interesting activities going on in the room so you don't get mobbed at the cooking table; and start cooking projects in a quiet low-key way with no loud announcements.

9. Have plenty of potholders (you can all make these another time).

10. Use extra-big bowls and pans to prevent spillovers — and have lots of stirring spoons to avoid grabbing.

11. Don't let children operate electric grinders, blenders, or mixers. One mistake can be too costly. (Besides, hand grinders, food mills, and egg beaters are more fun.)

A few other points to remember: Allow plenty of time for experiences along the way. Start cooking projects *only* when you're able to relax, accept a reasonable amount of mess, and keep the process fun without worrying too much about the product. Plan to have extra ingredients on hand for tastes and spills. Of course, every project starts with the time-honored custom of washing hands. But don't get overly worried about spoon-licking if the food is going to be cooked — after all, heat kills germs.

A final word about clean-up: it shouldn't be *final*. Incorporating it as part of the step-by-step process is not only worthwhile (we all know about dried eggs, batters, etc.), or sometimes necessary (if your equipment is as limited as ours) but can really be fun. Once when serving pancakes we had to borrow plates from the housekeeping corner, and each child after finishing his pancake was responsible for washing and drying his plate and having it ready for the next child. They all loved doing it.

One more important thing for teachers and parents to be aware of is that food is an emotional subject. Feeding children involves security and love and giving — and sometimes withdrawal, depriving, rewarding, and bribery. Some children may need to gorge themselves for a while, on sweets especially. Let them, and with the pressure off they will eventually ease up. Tensions can be released in cooking, too, by using physical rather than electrical energy whenever possible — grinding, mincing, hammering, kneading.

On the positive side, cooking can provide children with a tremendous sense of personal achievement by giving them a real point of entry into the adult world they try so hard to imitate. After all, they can only *pretend* to drive a car, have a baby, or make a sick person well. But they *really* can cook and produce real food which real people will really eat. In the light of all the other emotional/psychological connotations food has, think what a great sense of pride and accomplishment a child can get by cooking something for himself and someone he loves.

Adults need to recognize their own needs and fears connected with food — both eating and preparing it. Before starting a cooking project, teachers and parents might think about their own hang-ups. Cooking is an organized process, but you can still give the kids a chance to explore, play with food, eat some as they go along, and *even fail*, if they don't measure accurately or stir long enough. Why not try new ways of cooking yourself? Practice the night before, or suggest cooking as part of a teachers' workshop.

With cooking, as with most things, there are lots of approaches and no one right way. In this book are many of the ideas that have worked for us. We hope you'll try some of them and add plenty of your own.

by Liz Uraneck
Hap Tierney
Roz Ault
Jean Lokensgard

A NOTE ON INGREDIENTS

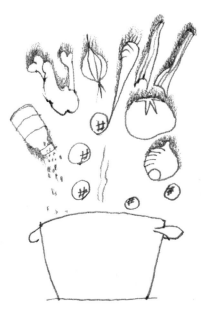

Most of the ingredients used in these recipes are readily available at the supermarket. A few items may necessitate a trip to a health-foods store. Some of the recipes, for example, will only work with noninstant-type powdered milk, which is not stocked in most regular grocery stores. This has an entirely different texture from instant dry milk powder — it is smoother and less grainy. Where the noninstant type is not specified, either kind may be used.

There are also two types of whole-wheat flour — regular and pastry. The whole-wheat pastry flour is preferred for baked goods where a lighter texture is desired. If you can't find it, you can approximate it by sifting regular whole-wheat flour and discarding the coarse bran. When white flour is used, the unbleached type is always nutritionally preferable.

Many of the recipes using chocolate call for unsweetened cocoa powder. Be sure you don't substitute the presweetened cocoa mixes. Many natural-foods cookbooks use carob powder instead of chocolate, but it doesn't taste the same, and unless you're allergic to chocolate there doesn't seem to be any convincing nutritional argument against it.

These substitution guidelines may be helpful if you wish to adapt other recipes:

Sweeteners. You may substitute ⅔ cup honey or molasses for each cup of sugar. Replace one fourth of the baking powder (if called for) with baking soda. Reduce liquid in recipe by 3 Tablespoons for every cup of honey or molasses. (Most baked goods will turn out better if you replace only part of the sugar, but some experimentation is necessary.) If honey crystallizes, put the jar in a pan of water and heat it very slowly (don't boil).

Flours. Substitute ⅞ cup whole-wheat flour for 1 cup white flour. Baked goods with 100 percent whole-wheat flour will not rise as high and will be coarser than those of white flour. If lightness and fine texture are crucial, replace only half the white flour, or replace 2 Tablespoons flour per cup with wheat germ.

The "Cornell formula" is another good way to add protein and other nutrients to white flour. When using flour, put in the bottom of each one-cup measure: 1 Tablespoon soy flour, 1 Tablespoon powdered milk, 1 Tablespoon wheat germ. Then fill the cup with sifted flour.

A CATALOG OF
COOKING EXPERIENCES

What happened when we made "My Teacher's Wedding Cake"

As a specific illustration of the varieties of experience involved in cooking, the teachers at Parents' Nursery School drew up this record of what actually went on one day when a group of children baked a cake (see the recipe on page 12).

Planning — what goes into a cake?
                discussion of various ingredients

Taking turns

Grinding (grain to flour)
Measuring
Pouring
Mixing
Stirring
Beating (with egg beaters)
Squeezing (lemon)

Tasting (along the way)
Smelling (spices, cake while baking)
Seeing and feeling changes (color and consistency
    of wheat when ground into flour)

Cleaning up (as part of process)

Walk to store to buy lemon for the frosting
    things observed along the way
    remembering what we came for, and finding it
    discussion of lemon and sugar, sweet versus
        sour

Timing — watching clock to see "if it's there yet"
    (the hands)

Counting — how many people, how many pieces

Discussion afterward of who did what — equal importance of each contribution

Spontaneous and orderly lining up on bench waiting for cake

Celebration of recent uncelebrated birthdays
singing
candles stuck in clay
tasting clay because it looked like chocolate

Eating!

Types of experience involved:
Motor: grinding, pouring, beating, squeezing
Sensory: tasting, smelling, touching, seeing
Social: taking turns, discussions, waiting, sharing, singing
Conceptual: measuring, counting, timing

INDEX

Parents' Nursery School in Cambridge, Mass., is a cooperative pre-school where parents and teachers work together to create a place for each child to grow and learn according to his/her own special strengths and needs. Although cooking is just one aspect of the school's program, under the direction of Liz Uraneck it became a tremendously exciting and rewarding one. Years before "natural foods" became a household word, Liz was grinding wheat with three- and four-year-olds to bake into bread and chopping vegetables from back-yard gardens to brew into huge pots of soup. Her example inspired other teachers and parents to contribute recipes and ideas — and of course, many of the best ideas came from the children themselves! Roz Ault, whose two sons were among Liz's culinary proteges, took on the job of writer/editor, and what evolved was this book — full of child-tested projects for happy cooking and good eating.

KIDS ARE NATURAL COOKS was first published privately in 1972 as a fund-raising project for the Parents' Nursery School. The original book has since been expanded and reillustrated but the proceeds continue to go to the school's education and scholarship program.